ᴜᴌ ᴌ7

D0166544

When Christmas
HURTS

Devotions of Hope

Patricia Acheson Wasylyna

WESTBOW
P R E S S®
A DIVISION OF THOMAS NELSON
& ZONDERVAN

WestBow Press books may be ordered through booksellers or by contacting:

WestBow Press
A Division of Thomas Nelson & Zondervan
1663 Liberty Drive
Bloomington, IN 47403
www.westbowpress.com
1 (866) 928-1240

ISBN: 978-1-9736-0404-4 (sc)
ISBN: 978-1-9736-0405-1 (hc)
ISBN: 978-1-9736-0403-7 (e)

Library of Congress Control Number: 2017915365

Print information available on the last page.

WestBow Press rev. date: 10/17/2017

Table of Contents

Introduction

Christmas can be a marvelous, enchanted, joyous time of year for healthy, cohesive families or when life is going smoothly and all is well in our world. However, it can also have the effect of a giant magnifying lens that parks itself over our life and practically screams out:

- Something is very wrong here.
- You are alone.
- You are different.
- Your family is a mess.
- He/she is gone.
- It's not the same.
- No one cares.
- You are broke.

Whatever the issue is, it becomes exposed and magnified, and the voices scream loud and clear throughout the season. The result is heartbreaking.

Psalm 27:13 says, "I would have lost heart, unless I had believed that I would see the goodness of the LORD in the land of the living." There came a point where I had "lost heart" concerning Christmas. The comparison between the celebrations I tried to create and the special Christmas memories I had from childhood was disheartening. Mix that with the disappointing reality of the way our culture has chosen to celebrate the season with all the commercialism and expectations and I felt overwhelmed. The home I grew up in was full of love, acceptance, and stability. Christmas was a wonderful, warm, exciting part of my childhood. There was no conflict, brokenness, or tension.

For years I held the same expectations of those childhood memories, only to be continually disappointed by the result of someone's attitude or actions destroying my dreams. There were also holidays overwhelmed by grief due to the absence or loss of a loved one and the pain of broken relationships. When you add in all the extra busyness and chaos that comes with the expectations we put on ourselves—and that others put on us to create the *perfect* Christmas—any excitement or anticipation for the holiday soon turns to dread and fear.

I have learned, over time, to turn elsewhere for the joy, wonder, and beauty of this season and look deep into the heart of God. This is the same God who loves us enough to send his Son to our world to be our teacher, example, and to open the way to unencumbered relationship with him. I need to be reminded of God's character which is loving, trustworthy, just, merciful, faithful, compassionate, and accepting. I need to look for the outpouring of his heart in my daily experiences. It's all around us, in people, in nature, in his Word, in moments of peace and joy. It can be very hard to discern during this season with all the bustle and busyness, but it is there.

How I wish Christmas could be celebrated differently, celebrated with a few days when everything slows down and our already busy lives can take a break, (a Sabbath) from our work, our activities, and our demands. A time when we can allow ourselves to "be still" and really commune with God. A time to reflect on the birth of our Savior and his sacrifice for us, and what it means in our lives. A time to be thankful for our blessings and fully enjoy family and friends without being rushed or distracted by often meaningless traditions demanding our time and energy to achieve some preconceived fantasy for the holiday. But that is not to be in the culture we live in. However, we can choose it for ourselves in some capacity. We can liberate ourselves from the chaos. We can learn to silence the voices of loneliness, anxiety, and despair. We can get off the wheel of expectations and perfection. We can choose.

My desire is that this devotional will help to silence those voices and wrap comfort and hope around the hurting, exposed places where fear and trepidation may cloud the thoughts of looming Christmas gatherings and celebrations. You will discover pathways of peace for those harried, stressful weeks of preparation while trying to meet all manner of expectations. I will challenge you to consider a change that will help you keep Christmas glorious without tearing at tender wounds and painful places in your heart—a revitalizing, liberating, God-glorifying change.

All Scripture was taken from, "The Spirit Filled Life Bible, New King James Version" unless otherwise noted.

All Biblical word definitions were taken from, "The New Strong's Exhaustive Concordance of the Bible." Unless otherwise noted.

The Tradition of Advent

This devotional is centered on the four weeks of Advent that precede Christmas. The word *Advent* means "coming into place" or "arrival." The season is focused on remembering the birth of Jesus in his first coming, the promise of redemption and hope, and the joyful expectation of his promised return in his second coming.

Originally, these four weeks were celebrated with a time of sorrowful repentance, reflection, and fasting—except for the fourth Sunday, which came to signify a time of joy because the fasting was nearly over. Over time, changes took place in the emphasis and symbolism. It is now celebrated as a time of joyful anticipation, hope, and thankful recognition of God's benevolent work through the life of Jesus. God's plan through Jesus brought us freedom from the power of sin and the ability to be partakers of God's divine influence through the Holy Spirit. Advent celebrates the fact that Christ has come, that he is present in our lives today, and that he will come again to bring peace and final restoration.

Advent begins on the fourth Sunday before Christmas Day, which is the Sunday closest to November 30. It ends on Christmas Eve. When Christmas Eve falls on a Sunday, it is counted as the fourth Sunday.

The tradition of the Advent Wreath holds a great deal of beautiful symbolism that can help us stay focused on the true meaning of Christmas. It gives us a very meaningful, devoted, yet simple way to observe and celebrate the season. The wreath is made of a circle of evergreen branches. Four candles are placed around the circle. Three of them are blue or purple, and one is pink or rose color. A white candle is placed in the center of the wreath. One blue or purple candle is lit at the beginning of the first week. The following Sunday, the first *two* candles are lit, and the progression continues until Christmas Eve or Christmas Day when the white candle is lit and all candles are now burning. The symbols of the wreath are as follows:

- **The Circle of the Wreath:** A reminder of God, his eternity, and endless mercy with no beginning and no end.
- **The Green of the Wreath:** Symbolizes our hope in God for newness, renewal, and eternal life.
- **The Light of the Candles:** The light of God coming into our world through Christ, bringing life and hope, and displacing darkness.
- **The Progression of Lighting the Candles:** Represents the waning darkness in the world as more and more of Christ's light is shed to overcome darkness.
- **Four Candles:** The four weeks of waiting during Advent which represents the four centuries between the time of Malachi's prophecy of Christ's coming and his birth.
- **The Blue or Purple Candles:** The color purple symbolizes royalty and blue symbolizes hope and waiting.
- **The Rose or Pink Candle:** Rose is the color of joy.
- **The White Candle:** Purity and righteousness.
- **The First Candle:** A time of expectation and HOPE.
- **The Second Candle:** The PEACE that is to come.
- **The Third Candle:** JOY for the promise is almost fulfilled.
- **The Fourth Candle:** God's LOVE for all mankind.

- **The Fifth and Center Candle:** Lit on Christmas Eve or Christmas Day to announce that the light of Christ has come into the world to fulfill the long awaited prophecies.

If you decide to include the Advent Wreath in your observance of Christmas, you can create your own tradition with it and be creative with its display. It's a great way to involve family or friends in a meaningful devotion during the season. The wreath could be placed at the family table or another central location. As the candles are lit each day, a passage of Scripture can be read and/or a devotion.

If you choose to use this devotional, you will find there are **Challenges** included for most of the days or weeks. I encourage you, and each person you are sharing the devotion time with, to engage in the challenges. Hopefully, this will cause you to be more fully aware of the "Reason for the Season" and give you a new outlook on possible ways to experience and share the love of Christ. A time can be set during ongoing devotion time to follow up on how each individual has met the challenge or experienced a "God Moment" that day or week.

I have also included, **Further Reading** at the end of each devotion. As time allows, avail yourself of these Scriptures to expound on the topics and nurture yourself further in God's Word. If time is short, go back to these passages at another time. The more we fill ourselves with God's Word, the deeper we come to know him.

There are endless possibilities in how the Advent Wreath or this devotional can be used to add meaning and honor to your Christmas. Whether you are alone or part of a family or circle of friends, I believe you will find meaning and peace in the symbolism and simplicity if you choose to adopt it.

May God pour his divine influence on your heart and reveal himself to you in ways that bring you hope, peace, comfort, and joy in this season of celebrating the coming of his Son who came to us as "Immanuel, God with us."

Week One

HOPE

Day One
Get Settled

*But as for me, I trust in You, O Lord; I say, "You are
my God." My times are in Your hand.*
~ Psalm 31:14–15

The first of the four Advent candles is lit on the Sunday of the
fourth week before Christmas. This candle signifies hope and
expectation.

What is hope? Hope is not the same as desire or wishing.
Wishing is when we are engaged in looking for a particular outcome
based on our own desires or thoughts on the matter at hand. True
hope doesn't concern itself with the outcome. It is based on the
confidence and assurance that someone or something has proven
to be trustworthy in the past and will be again. It is born out of
faith and trust.

Hebrews 11:1 tells us that faith is the substance of our hope. In
other words, faith is what hope is made of. A footnote in my Bible
says, "Faith is established conviction concerning things unseen
and settled expectation of future reward." I like that term, *settled
expectation*. It's like having an established conviction and settled
expectation of flicking a switch, believing the light will come on.
That's the kind of hope God encourages us to have.

God's Word has over 125 places where the word *hope* is used, and it nearly always refers to our hope being in him. This is the only place we can confidently place our hope because of who he is and his unconditional love for us. The holidays can cause us to place our hope in things that will disappoint and cause us to make choices that create stress and unnecessary busyness. They can also lead us to place unrealistic expectations on people and experiences. We often create fantasies of how we want things to turn out or how we want people to behave. That kind of hope can result in discouragement and turn our focus to lamenting over our disappointment.

Lamentations 3:20–24 says, "My soul still remembers and sinks within me. This I recall to my mind, therefore I have hope. Through the LORD'S mercies we are not consumed, because His compassions fail not. They are new every morning. Great is Your faithfulness. 'The LORD is my portion,' says my soul, 'therefore I hope in Him.'"

Yes, the Lord is our portion. The word *portion* here means a distribution or inheritance. This means the Lord himself is given to us to fulfill our need with his attributes. His attributes are unchanging, fulfilling, and sustaining. God is faithful, loving, compassionate, merciful, just, powerful, and wise. As we exercise faith and trust in him, he is able and promises to empower us with those same attributes, helping us to go through difficult times— including difficult holidays—with better attitudes and better outcomes.

Perhaps you are facing Christmas this year with the absence of someone you love. Maybe you are dreading certain interactions with troubled relationships or just overwhelmed with the thought of all the added busyness. If you are struggling in any area, your best hope is in trusting God because his compassion never fails. He has the ability to give us what we need even when we don't know what we need. Our situations may or may not change, and things may not turn out the way we wish, but we can be filled and empowered with his influence and be at peace as we trust him for the outcome.

Quote: "Faith is not a bridge over troubled waters but a pathway through them" (The Spirit Filled Life Bible, footnote to Hebrews 11:35–38).

This Week's Hope Challenge: Be intentional as you rise each morning to start the day with thoughts and words of hope. If you are feeling defeated in an area of your life, exercise faith in the Father's love for you, his power and ability to sustain you, and be with you in your situation. Choose to have a settled expectation of his presence, guidance, and intervention throughout your day and for your circumstances. Record any ways God gives you inspirations of hope and share them with a friend or family member.

Further Reading: Hebrews 11

Day Two
Blindsided

Hope deferred makes the heart sick, but when the
desire comes it is a tree of life.
~ Proverbs 13:12

There is a day in my history that I refer to as the Black Christmas. That day still casts a shadow over my memories of past Christmas days, attempting to eclipse the peace and contentment of today. When it does, I try to remember the hope in what God taught me through that experience. I spent several years pretty much a wreck in the weeks preceding Christmas. Once October evolved into November, I would be overcome by a heavy sense of dread, worry, and fear over the upcoming celebrations. Imaginations of results from unpredictable dispositions nagged at my thoughts. Sadness from the ache that came over me for those who would be absent and missed, and for what was lost, was overwhelming.

The agony of being caught in the middle of broken relationships, resentments, and bad attitudes can be difficult regardless of the time of year, but it magnifies with the expectations of happy holidays. Strife and division seem more intense. The heaviness of rejection, silent treatment, or tension can hang in the air so thick that it seems to wrap itself around one's heart in a suffocating vice of pain and uneasiness and clouds all joyful Christmas anticipation.

For many years, this was my pre-Christmas experience. The only thing I looked forward to were the hours we would gather as a family, with my brothers, sisters, parents, nieces, and nephews. Here I felt safe and loved and had some semblance of the heart of Christmas. Here I felt relief and a glimmer of the warmth, fun, and wonder of the Christmases I experienced as a child.

One particular season, I was determined not to let the usual dread consume me. I would instead trust God for the outcome. I decided to turn every fearful thought into trusting God to do whatever it took for the days to be good, for people to be thoughtful and kind, and for my own heart to be steady and more peaceful. So I trusted God, and all the while, I was imagining a good Christmas.

Christmas Day came. Even though we weren't all together, and my heart ached for the missing one, it was peaceful and any tension bearable. The day progressed in a fairly pleasant way. I thought we would make it, that we would look back and say, "It was good." But attitudes changed unexpectedly, and my fears became reality in an outburst that left me feeling traumatized.

I felt emotionally weak and shaken, and I lay in my bed that night trying to make sense of the storm that had just ripped through my heart. And I was so mad at God. My heart cried out, "What is up with this, God? Where were you? I trusted you!"

For days I felt betrayed and abandoned by God. My faith was broken. I struggled to make sense of it all. At some point, almost reluctantly, I turned to God's Word because that's where I go when I'm feeling lost. The words of Jesus in Matthew 7:6 rose off the page: "Do not give what is holy to the dogs; nor cast your pearls before swine, lest they trample them under their feet, and turn and tear you in pieces."

Suddenly, God showed me that I hadn't really been trusting

him; I had been trusting in my own fantasy of how I wanted things to turn out and how I wanted people to act. God gives free will, but he doesn't control others. God was tenderly saying to me, "Don't give what is special and valuable into the hands of humanity who may or may not share your heart and your values. Don't place your dreams or hopes with human hearts that are unpredictable, uninterested, or uncaring. They may destroy them and cause you great pain."

That is exactly what I had done. I had put my hope in the fact that all would be great if everyone executed and shared my expectation of a happy and peaceful Christmas. I was counting on God to make people act the way I wanted. My thoughts turned to Psalm 62:5–8, "My soul *wait silently* for God *alone*, for my expectation is from Him" (italics mine).

My soul had been far from silent. I was busy planning and preparing my dream, instructing God in my own way, and preparing for my outcome. Gently, God was making it clear. My expectation can safely be in him alone. What can I expect from God? That he will never leave me or forsake me (see Deuteronomy 31:6, Joshua 1:5, and Hebrews 13:5). He will sustain, comfort, and strengthen me and give me rest, peace, and joy. His character is always loving, always faithful, always just; therefore he is always safe (see scripture references below).

How can we keep our expectations in him alone? By keeping our focus on him and on his promises and unchanging love for us. We must silence our minds from the barrage of thoughts, fears, and fantasies that distract us by letting those thoughts go. Silence them by replacing them with positive, believing thoughts and scriptural truth. Practice focusing on him and who he promises to be, not the outcome of your choosing. He knows our hearts and our desires, and he knows what's best for us. We must be willing to trust him to be God in our lives and to be the source of our hope. Romans 15:13

(God's Word translation) says, "May God, the source of hope, fill you with joy and peace through your faith in Him. Then you will overflow with hope by the power of the Holy Spirit." It is through our faith in him, persevering to keep our hearts pressed to his, and holding on to his character and his promises, that the Holy Spirit sustains and magnifies our hope.

Today's Hope Challenge: Is there a situation or fear that has you in its grip? Is there an area where you may be relying on the wrong source or your own imaginations for the resolution or hope? Begin to turn your thoughts away from the outcome to the promises of God and his love for you. Pray for his peace, love, healing, provision, and truth to permeate the situation. Trust God with the outcome.

Further Reading: Psalm 55:22, Matthew 11:28, John 14:27, Psalm 126:5–6, and Psalm 91

Day Three

Expectations

Expectations of myself, those that others put on me, and those I put on others, became traps during the Christmas season. I would find myself in a frenzy of decorating, baking, buying, shopping, wrapping, cleaning, attending, appeasing, obliging ... until I was tired, frazzled, rushed, defeated, angry, resentful, fearful, discouraged, and most of all—much to the satisfaction of the enemy of my soul—distracted.

Realizing I was totally and completely distracted from the real reason for celebrating Christmas, it became evident that I needed to ask myself a very important question concerning all of this activity. The Question? "Why?" What is motivating me to shop till I drop or bake till I'm blue? Why am I decorating under duress or wrapping till I'm weary? Is this how God wants me to commemorate the love gift of Christ in my life? Is my motivation birthed from thankfulness and love for him and others, or from pride, perfection, or fear of disappointing someone? Are my activities adding to the glory of Christmas or to the chaos?

I started to go down the list of expectations and activities and realized I needed to seriously contemplate the value of all the things that get added to my schedule this time of year. I needed to find out what was meaningful and enriching and what was pure activity, for activity's sake, that only added chaos.

A grain of wheat contains the edible kernel that is valuable for food. It also contains an outer covering called the chaff that is discarded because it impairs the digestion of the nourishing wheat. There are many Christmas traditions and activities that are part of our typical celebrations. How many of them are just chaff, preventing us from enjoying and benefitting from the ones that truly reflect the true Spirit and meaning of Christmas?

As I went down my list of expectations and activities of the season, I realized I needed to separate the wheat from the chaff by keeping what was truly valuable and letting the rest fall away. My list of wheat and chaff will, most likely, look very different from yours because we are all unique in what is valuable to us and what motivates us. Many of the activities of the season, in and of themselves, are mostly good. Deciding if they are good for *us* and why we engage in them is key. Here is an example from my own experience as I began to sort this out.

Like most families, we always put up a Christmas tree when I was growing up. It was a family affair to string the lights, pull out the ornaments, and place them on the tree together. Usually, a snack and some hot chocolate were part of the fun as well. As I moved the tradition into my own family, we did the same. Although my husband preferred some quiet time in front of the television, my boys were excited to participate and enjoyed pulling the ornaments out of the boxes, as I did, and reminiscing about their significance to us. Each child had their own special ornament or two and they made sure to find a special spot for it among the branches. It was a fun and happy time and we would enjoy making a day of it.

As the years progressed, my young men's enthusiasm for adorning the tree declined in exchange for testosterone and meaningful activities like sports and friends. I found myself to be solo in dragging out the tree, making a day of putting it together, rearranging furniture, and stringing lights. Alone again, I would spend another day unwrapping ornaments and musing over where to place them on the tree. All the while, I was fighting feelings of sadness, remembering years past when we had so much fun doing it together. In those days I reveled in the excitement of my family, now replaced by excuses of why they didn't want to help—the trials of being the only female in a houseful of males.

During one particular Christmas season, our tree came crashing to the floor after being accosted by an airborne detergent bottle, bursting open and oozing its contents over the tree. It was a horrible mess and a stressful event.

So, with all these changes, the adorning of the tree took on a different sentiment. I found resentment and disappointment lurking in the process and a sadness that overwhelmed me at times. The labor and time involved became a burden when not shared with joyful participants. We would forget to light the tree for days, and no one even noticed. I asked myself, "Why am I doing this? Is this activity motivated by love? Is it adding to the glory of Christmas or the chaos?"

I knew it was adding to the chaos in my own heart. The rest of the family wasn't interested enough to help or enjoy the tree once it was in place. It seemed the only reason I could find for doing it was the proverbial, "That's what we've always done."

So I have decided to let it go and have replaced it with a simple, yet meaningful, display that reflects the real message of Christmas. I created an advent wreath that takes up residence in a central place in our home during the four weeks before Christmas.

The wreath is set on a red cloth. Four candles circle it and I display the words *Hope, Peace, Joy,* and *Love* at their base. A white candle is placed in the center of the wreath and has the words *Immanuel, God With Us* beneath it. A large angel stands behind the wreath and smaller ones flank either side. Garland and miniature lights frame the display.

Arranging the display brings me peace and joy, and I feel like I am honoring God, celebrating the birth of Jesus, and creating a reminder for all who see it. I can't pass by it in my home without feeling a sense of honor and thankfulness to God. An added benefit is that it takes less than an hour to set up, and I don't have to rearrange the room.

I get a little flak from some people for not putting up a tree, but when I share the heart and message behind the wreath and my decision to use it, I perceive that they are relating to my alteration of tradition.

There are other traditions I have given up or modified as well. I keep decorating simple. I don't send Christmas cards to very many people and have cut back on Christmas baking, shopping, and gifts exchanged. The favorite cookies I bake and the gifts I buy are more special because I have the time to put my heart into everything I do. There is also more time for reflection, reading, and staying focused on the reason we celebrate.

Perhaps you need to ask, "Why?" Are you participating in traditions or demands that cause more chaos than joy? Do some activities rip at tender wounds or replay painful memories? It may be time to let them go. If possible, replace them with something that soothes your soul, brings you peace, honors the Lord, and strengthens you in his love. Let the trappings go and you may discover a treasure. Yes, there is hope for a simple and meaningful Christmas.

Today's Hope Challenge: Create your own list of wheat and chaff activities that are part of your traditional Christmas celebration. Talk with your spouse and/or children (if you are part of a family) and get their input. Let go of traditions that cause stress and become a burden. Developing new, simple traditions can be fun and will set you free from those empty activities that can cause chaos or painful memories.

Further reading: Romans 12:2, Luke 10:38-42, Proverbs 17:1, Proverbs 15:16-17, Matthew 6:19-21

Day Four

A Sound Mind

For God has not given us a spirit of fear, but of power
and of love and of a sound mind.
~ 2 Timothy 1:7

If faith is the substance of our hope, then fear—the opposite of faith—is the substance of our worry, anxiety, dread, depression and hopelessness. In other words, hope is made from faith. Negative emotions are made from fear.

As I have shared earlier, the months before Christmas were overshadowed with a nagging dread and fear for me. A fear that intensified with each passing day. All I really wanted to do was escape to some peaceful, warm beach somewhere—alone—and avoid the holiday altogether. My fears revolved around broken, bitter, relationships, and the tug-of-war that resulted from them. It was emotionally draining. Anything that was normally difficult with relationships seemed to intensify and become even more difficult during the Christmas season. I dreaded the busyness and countless expectations that made things even more stressful and exhausting.

Maybe you have similar issues in your family, your work place, your church, or with another group of people you share a part of

13

your life with. Perhaps you become stressed and burned out from all the busyness as well. How do we handle this? How can we restore a sense of hope rather than dread?

Personally, I had to come face-to-face with my codependent thinking. Codependency can be defined as having your emotions and feelings continually tied to the behavior of others. I could have been the poster child for codependency. The behavior of others had me tied up in knots and running in circles.

The verse from 2 Timothy above has been a lifeline for me. It reminds me that I have power over my own reactions to the way people choose to behave. The power to change or control other people is not within my means, but I *can* control my responses. I do have choices such as not letting the behavior of others affect my stability, and not accepting blame or false guilt. I can choose to do things differently or walk away from stressful or unhealthy interactions if necessary, especially when it's the wise thing to do. It's my choice to utilize the power we all have through the Holy Spirit that can give us strength and courage to say no when we need to, or yes when we want to.

What we choose to believe, or how we choose to react to a given situation, ultimately determines the outcome's effect on us. If our belief system is empowered with truth, love, and faith from the Holy Spirit, it will greatly impact the outcome of those negative situations. "And we know that all things (*the event*) work together for good (*outcome*) to those who love God." (*belief system*) Romans 8:28. (Italics mine) I'm not saying the outcome won't be messy—or even horrid—but utilizing the power God has given us will make a difference in how it affects us.

God has also given us his Spirit of love. It is another aspect of his grace, a character trait he possesses and is willing to give to us. How amazing. I am truly grateful because my own attempts to love, especially in negative situations, often fail miserably. Fortunately, we can continually ask God to renew our hearts and minds with his love. Through that love we can be reassured in times of fear that his love is never failing, that he is with us and will not abandon us. 1 John 4:18 reminds us that his "perfect love casts out fear." Isaiah 41:13 states, "For I, the LORD your God, will hold your right hand, saying to you, 'Fear not, I will help you.'"

The Holy Spirit can also give us a "sound mind." The term *sound mind* is translated, "safe thinking." Our thinking can really mess us up, and in that respect, can be far from safe for our stability and our mental and emotional health. God's Word tells us to take our thoughts captive by focusing on how Jesus chose obedience and perseverance through unimaginable pain and suffering, "bringing every thought into captivity to the obedience of Christ" (2 Corinthians 10:5) I don't believe this verse is telling us to make our thoughts obedient. Personally, I think that's impossible. I know thoughts pop into my head with no effort on my part, and I can no more control them than I can my heartbeat. The key is what I do with those thoughts once they surface that makes the difference.

As Christ went to the cross, he exercised safe thinking. He completely put his trust in God, asking for God's will to be done, in spite of his request to save him from the agony ahead. The cross was meant, by the Romans and Satan, to be a defeat and a place of shame for Jesus and all he stood for. Yet Hebrews 12:2 tells us that he *endured* the cross and *despised* the shame of it. That word *endure* in the Greek language means: "stand firm, persevere, (not passive resignation or patience) but active, energetic, resistance." The word *despise* in the Greek means: "to think against."

Wow. Christ made a decision to fully trust God, and, in doing so, God gave him the power to stand firm and resist the evil intent of the cross. Jesus was empowered to *think against* any shame the enemy intended, in order to fall into obedience to God's plan and purpose for him and accomplish the victory of the cross.

As Christ followers, we are asked to have the mind of Christ. Because we are empowered by the Holy Spirit, we have the ability and can choose to exercise this kind of thinking to persevere and actively resist thoughts that can keep us from having a sound mind—a mind that is not frazzled and anxious but exercising faith. A mind not full of anger or frustration, but enveloped in peace. Depression and hopelessness can be replaced by truth and stability. How?

Here are a few suggestions:

- Reciting and declaring Scripture that speaks truth to your situation.
- Sifting your thoughts through a test of truth. Is there substantial truth to what I am thinking? Or am I believing or ruminating over a lie or an assumption?
- Renewing your mind with truth and safe thinking. Take your thoughts captive before they begin to mess with your peace.

Today's Hope Challenge: If there is something that has you going down the "fear" road or you find yourself distracted and worried by it, use the suggestions above to resists the negative thoughts and the spiral of discouragement. You will find that your day will open up to more hopeful feelings and more effective interactions. Fear and discouragement paralyze us. The truth sets us free.

Further reading: Psalm 18:28-33, Psalm 27:1, Psalm 28:7-9, Psalm 56, Psalm 57:1, Psalm 138:7-8, Proverbs 29:25

Day Five
Wait

Wait on the LORD; be of good courage, and He shall
strengthen your heart; wait, I say, on the LORD!
~ Psalm 27:14

Waiting is hard. There are things I have prayed for and hoped for that passing time has allowed doubt to creep in about their fulfillment. In those times I find my hope wavering, sometimes even changing to despair or anger.

God asks us to wait, not for what we hope for, not to have our expectations met, but he asks us to wait on *him*. The word *wait* in this verse has an unusual meaning in the original Hebrew language. It means, "to bind together by twisting, to expect." This meaning indicates that we are to bind ourselves together with the Lord and expect him to be God.

In my mind, it is similar to how a husband and wife bind themselves to each other, emotionally, physically, and materially, and expect the other to fulfill the covenant and blessing of their marriage. They are "waiting" on each other for the promises of their covenant to be a reality in their life together.

As we bind ourselves to God in full devotion and trust, he pours his grace (his divine influence and attributes) into our hearts and our circumstances. When we ask for his help, he strengthens and empowers us. That is grace. The Greek word for grace is *charis*. It means: "a favor, gift, benefit, the divine influence upon the heart and its reflection in life." This definition clarifies that God will give us the needed benefit and influence for the situation we are in. It may not necessarily be what we want, but he will provide what is needed.

Our circumstances may not change, or our expectations be met, but we can be assured of more courage, strength, or help where we are lacking.

The 20th chapter of 2 Chronicles is an account of God's divine influence as people bound themselves to him in trust and belief. A huge army was poised to attack the land that Jehoshaphat was reigning over. He turned immediately to the Lord and sought his help, then gathered the people to fast and pray. After reminding himself of examples of God's power and help in other circumstances, he made a declaration to God of his trust and belief in God's ability to help them, admitting the lack of power that he and his people possessed in the situation.

God then gave instructions and told them not to be afraid. He promised that the enemy would be defeated if they would position themselves where he told them and stand still. They were not to try and take the enemy and wouldn't even have to fight—the Lord would fight for them. They believed and went to the battleground praising God for his mercy and goodness even before the battle began. Indeed, God sent an ambush of other attackers against their enemy and they were defeated. There are several important principles in this account of victory.

- Jehoshaphat turned to God for help.
- He enlisted the prayers of the people.
- He stirred up his faith by remembering.

- He declared his belief that God could save them.
- He admitted his lack of power over the situation.
- He obeyed God's instruction and believed God's word to him.
- He praised God and was obedient to God's instruction to send people in front of the battle lines to praise God as they moved forward.

God admonished them to not fear or be dismayed. All of Jehoshaphat's actions dispelled any fear that might have overwhelmed them. He bound himself to God in devotion and trust and waited on God to act.

As we head into challenging situations or handle difficult circumstances, these are principles that we can exercise as well. God is willing and able to help us in times of need.

Today's Hope Challenge: Wait on the Lord by implementing the principles described above in an area that you might be struggling with, or share them with someone who may be struggling.

Further reading: 2 Chronicles chapter 20, Psalm 25:4-5, Psalm 130:5-6, Psalm 33:20, Isaiah 40:31

Day Six
Go Deep

This hope we have as an anchor of the soul, both sure and steadfast, and which enters the Presence behind the veil.
~ Hebrews 6:19

What *is* this hope that we have? Let's unpack the rest of this section of Scripture above to find out. I am using the Amplified version of the Bible for this text to give us some added help. This version uses additional words that define and explain various parts of the original text. You will find the additional words in brackets.

Hebrews 6:13-19:

- **Vs. 13:** "For when God made the promise to Abraham, He swore [an oath] by Himself, since He had no one greater by whom to swear,"
- **Vs. 14:** "saying, 'I will surely bless you and I will surely multiply you.'"
- **Vs.15** "And so, having patiently waited, he realized the promise [in the miraculous birth of Isaac, as a pledge of what was to come from God]."

- **Vs. 16:** "Indeed men swear [an oath] by one greater than themselves, and with them [in all disputes] the oath serves as confirmation [of what has been said] and is an end of the dispute."
- **Vs.17:** "In the same way God, in His desire to show to the heirs of the promise the unchangeable nature of His purpose, intervened and guaranteed it with an oath,"
- **Vs. 18:** "So that by two unchangeable things [His promise and His oath] in which it is impossible for God to lie, we who have fled [to Him] for refuge would have strong encouragement and indwelling strength to hold tightly to the hope set before us."
- **Vs. 19:** "This hope [this confident assurance] we have as an anchor of the soul [it cannot slip and it cannot breakdown under whatever pressure bears upon it]—a safe and steadfast hope that enters within the veil [of the heavenly temple, that most Holy Place in which the very presence of God dwells]."

This hope that we have is the assurance that God will perform the many promises he has made to us in his Word. He cannot lie.

Have you ever been hit so hard with a situation or news that rocked you so much you couldn't even imagine going on? Something so devastating you couldn't fathom how life could possibly continue with any element of stability or happiness? Perhaps it's a financial crisis, an illness, divorce, or the death of a loved one who won't be with you this Christmas or in the days and years to come. The future looms dark, empty, and uncertain. Hope fails you and seems untrustworthy.

It's hard to even gather the strength to hope in times like these. For certain, hope can be untrustworthy and disappointing if we place it, or anchor it, in people or things that are neither capable nor empowered to sustain it. People, jobs, money, plans, and material things, can and will disappoint us.

In 2000, my mom, full of vibrant health and vitality, died suddenly and tragically. I spoke to her on the phone that day. She was happy and healthy, and we made plans to get together that evening. Only a few hours later she was gone ... forever. She would no longer be a part of this life with us. No good-byes or final words ... just gone.

Her sudden and unexpected passing rocked my world to the core. There are no words for the depth of pain or the grief that swallowed me. I questioned God and got no answers. I was angry with him and felt betrayed. To cast hope in any direction seemed completely pointless. The thought of being hopeful was mocking and painful. I wanted to turn my back on God and run. But to where? To whom? I didn't know, I just wanted relief from the agony of this empty, dark, painful, hopeless place. But there was nowhere to run to and no person who could relieve my suffering.

I eventually made a conscious choice. Even though my trust in God was deeply shaken and nearly nonexistent at that point, I knew somewhere deep within me, that he was my only chance for hope of any kind. Although at that point, I could not begin to understand or trust his actions or inaction, I chose to trust his character. I coined this "raw trust." Trust that simply relies solely on *who* God is and his attributes of love, faithfulness, power, and goodness. It was as if I were dangling over a sea of nothingness, clutching desperately with one hand to a lifeline that connected me to those attributes in him.

When a boat is being tossed and tortured by a ravaging sea, the only recourse is to set the anchor and ride out the storm. At that point, your hope of life and safety lies completely in the strength and greatness of the anchor. I was the boat and God was the anchor. Thankfully, his hold proved great enough and strong enough to sustain me through that horrific time in my life. Eventually, over time, I was able to grasp that lifeline with both hands until, gradually, peace began to come.

When our world is turned upside down, coming to a place of peace, with hope restored, relies fully on the choice we make in what we use for our anchor and who holds it. God alone is fully capable. We must choose him.

Reviewing verse 18 of the scripture in Hebrews 6 in the new King James Version, it says, "That by two immutable things, in which it is impossible for God to lie, we might have strong consolation who have fled for refuge to lay hold of the hope set before us." *Strong consolation.* The word consolation in Greek is, *paraklesis* meaning, "to come alongside, give comfort, encouragement." The word *paraklete* means "a strengthening presence." How amazing! Can't we all use a strengthening, comforting, presence?

Perhaps you are going through a very devastating time or place of crisis during this holiday. As believers, we have access to the strengthening presence and comfort of God but we must choose to reach for it and hold on. I pray that you will have the strength and courage to place your hope in the assuring hold of God's character and be strengthened by his comforting, empowering, and encouraging presence.

Today's Hope Challenge: Feeling rocked? Go deep and hold on to the promises of God's strengthening presence. Write out some of the scripture truths below, or other promises from God's word and recite them to yourself often to encourage hope and faith in who God promises to be for you.

No big waves in your life? Express your thankfulness. Ask yourself if there is a place or situation in your life where you can go deeper in your faith in God.

Further Reading: Psalm 9:9, Psalm 37:24, Psalm 57:1, Psalm 73:26, Psalm 94:18-19, Isaiah 43: 1-3, Nahum 1:7, Hebrews 10:23

Day Seven
New Beginnings

Do not remember the former things, nor consider the things of old. Behold, I will do a new thing.
~ Isaiah 43: 18-19a

There's something very energizing, exciting, and revitalizing about new things: A new car, a new house, a new experience, the first spring flower, a newborn baby, or even a new book.

What is it that sparks that thrill in us for newness? I think its hope—hope for something that will take us beyond the routine and the mundane and refresh us with contemplations of possibilities, opportunities, and the assurance of a continuum of the good things in life.

I'm a writer and I journal. I love the delight of a new journal in my hands ... all those empty pages waiting for new experiences, new thoughts, and new episodes of life yet to come. It sparks hope in me for pleasant things and good times. Unfortunately, these exciting feelings of the "new" are all temporal and fleeting. We don't have the ability to grasp and hold on to them. They ebb and flow in and out of our lives enough to keep us encouraged and hopeful, and we are grateful for them.

In this journey of life, we continually search for newness to awaken our spirit and distract our hearts from the mundane and life's pain, disappointment, or despair. Maybe it explains all the shoes in my closet. It can lead us down a path to debt or time deprivation. Deep down, it's our *heart* that is longing for renewal and these superficial things only bring an illusion of satisfying that longing.

Christmas is a celebration of the birth of Jesus into our world, the One who came with a *new* message, and—I might add—not a popular one. He came with a message that would bring new hope, new life, and a new start for any who would accept it. Unfortunately, many were not willing to give up their familiar traditions and ways of thinking ... and they missed out.

The message of Jesus is everlasting and not circumstantial. It offers a personal renewal of heart and soul. Newness that satisfies continually. Jesus' life, death, and resurrection gives us hope of being a *new creation* as we place our trust and belief in him, living our life following him and seeking his plan for our lives. We are a new creation because he promises that as we trust him we will be empowered by his own Spirit.

"Therefore, if anyone is in Christ, he is a new creation; old things have passed away; behold all things have become new." (2 Corinthians 5:17).

Anytime we have the opportunity to experience something new, we have to make some choices. We have to be willing to let go of the old or negative things to experience the new. We wouldn't be able to enjoy a new house until we moved out of our old house, making the effort to go through the process of buying and moving into the new one. The opportunities for fun and new experiences pass us by unless we decide to get off the couch, leave our comfort zone, and go for it. The thrill and joy of a newborn baby brings something excitingly new to witness at every turn. However, if we are paralyzed by fear of something bad happening to him or her, or being overwhelmed by lack of confidence in our parenting skills, we will miss out on unbelievable joy.

Jesus said in Matthew 9:17 that you can't put new wine into an old wineskin because the fermentation activity of the new wine will cause the old wineskin to burst and spill the wine. Neither the wine nor the wineskin will be any good. Both are destroyed. He gave this illustration in context of a question the disciples had asked him about a law of regular fasting. Jesus' reply was basically saying that you can't enjoy the newness and freedom of the gospel message by holding on to the legalistic practices of Judaism. One foot on either side of the fence just leaves you sitting on the fence, going nowhere.

It's easy to stay in bondage because it's comfortable or familiar, or we're fearful of rejection or some other outcome. The truth is we have to let go of the past, in most cases, in order to experience new beginnings. I heard a quote recently that says it well: "Often one thing must end in order for a new thing to have a chance to live" (unknown). This is true when it comes to our faith as well. We have to decide if we are going to be an observer or a follower of Christ. Being a true follower requires dying to our own will and agenda and being completely surrendered to God's plan for our life. Are we going to let things of our material world or monetary pursuits occupy too much of our time and energy? Will we let go of the frantic race for "more" and live unencumbered within a simpler lifestyle? Always choices. Our hope lies within our ability to choose the best and, most definitely, to rely on the Holy Spirit to lead us in our choosing.

Things we may need to let go of could involve our preparation and celebration of Christmas. It could be the way we've always handled a relationship, or the activities and traditions we've always maintained. I can remember how frazzled and impatient I could get with people and situations because of all the demands I placed on myself during the holiday season. It left me with frayed nerves and no joy. For me, choosing some new and simpler ways to celebrate, and letting go of some old ones, created more time, more peace, and more sanity.

In Matthew 5:14 Jesus tells us we are "the light of the world." In Ephesians 5:8 it says that we are to "Walk as children of light." Shouldn't our light shine even brighter this time of year? Jesus goes on to say that people don't put their light under a basket if they want it to give light to those around them. You may not be walking around with a basket on your head, but you could very well be enveloped in a cloud of deadlines, expectations, stress, and fears that hide any light that might be buried under all of it. It's impossible to shine as a light when I'm standing in yet another line, nervously tapping my foot and sighing with a scowl on my face that is sending the non-verbal message of, "I don't have time for you. I've got things to do. I've got to keep moving." We have no idea the impact that a smile, a kind exchange of words, or a little bit of our full attention might mean in someone's life.

So whatever area of your life you might need to let go of—past ways or thoughts, traditions or habits—be bold. Choose a new way that will bring freedom and refreshing. Watch it spill over onto those around you.

Let go and let your light shine.

Today's Hope Challenge: Ask God to show you any area where you might need to let go or let something end. Think of ways you can shine that extra light you'll have.

Further Reading: Isaiah 43:18-19, Jeremiah 31:31-34, Matthew 9:14-17, Colossians 3:9-10, Revelation 21:3-5

Week Two

PEACE

Day One
Jesus

Seek peace and pursue it.
~ Psalm 34:14 b

The second Advent candle is lit on this day. It signifies peace.

Peace. What does the word bring to your mind? A quiet walk in the woods? Reveling in the sights and sounds of a gentle waterfall? Listening to the rhythmical crashing of waves on the beach? A quiet, comfy respite with couch, blanket, and a good book? Or maybe just the cessation of noise, demands, and deadlines?

Each of us will have a different answer based on our need at the moment and what things soothe our soul. One of the meanings of peace, as stated by Merriam-Webster.com is, "Freedom from disquieting or oppressive thoughts or emotions. A state of tranquility or quiet." The biblical meaning of peace is much broader and reveals a heartwarming aspect of God's love for us. It may change your way of thinking about peace, as it did mine.

The Hebrew word for *peace* (used in the Old Testament) is, *shalom.* It means, "safe in mind and body, full, to be complete, to make amends, restore, finish."

The Greek word for *peace* (used in the New Testament) is, *eirene.* It means, "quiet, rest, to join, set at one again."

Let these words sink in deep. Both languages hold similar meanings. Most amazing is the indication of being complete, full, restored, and safe. What comforting and calming words to bathe our thoughts. Even more interesting are the aspects of "to join" and "to set at one again." At one? With what or whom? Joined? Again? Intriguing, and yet that is what God's Word tells us that he does for us.

- "For it pleased the Father that in Him (Jesus) all the fullness (of God) should dwell, and by Him (Jesus) to reconcile all things to Himself, (God) by Him, (Jesus), whether things on earth or things in heaven, having made peace (join, set as one, complete, safe) through the blood of His cross." Colossians 1: 19-20 (parentheses mine)
- "And this One (Jesus) shall be peace." Micah 5:5 (parentheses mine)
- "For He Himself is our peace, who has made both one, and has broken down the middle wall of separation." Ephesians 2:14

Jesus *is* our peace because he came to make us one again with God. He came to restore us to God's originally intended relationship with us. A place where we can be connected to God and be recipients of his influence. The grace that gives us qualities and stability beyond our own effort and make up. God gives us the ability to see beyond our chaos and our struggle with the assurance that we are not alone but one with him. When our thoughts and emotions are entwined with his, we are at one, at peace, in any situation.

This is no easy task, no automatic response. It requires choice, focus, diligence, and, most of all, faith and trust. Fear and doubt will attempt to dissuade us from our goal of intimacy and peace. We continually fight against those combatants of our serenity, but we have promises to hold on to. Our faith and trust will not go unrewarded. "You will keep him in perfect peace whose mind is stayed on You, because he trusts in You" (Isaiah 26:3).

It is trust that keeps our mind stayed on God. Choosing to trust. As we celebrate Christmas, let us keep in mind that the peace Jesus brought to us in his coming, is more than just freedom from disturbance or chaos. It is more than our picture of tranquility and rest. It is a lasting reunion with the Father and the divine benefits of that relationship.

This Week's Peace Challenge: Celebrate the peace that is available to you and all who follow Jesus. Pursue that connection with the Father that brings fullness and rest. Be an ambassador of the peace given to you through him. Pass it on.

Further reading: John 14:27, John 17:20-23, Romans 5:1-2, 2 Peter1:2, James 3:18, 2Corinthians 13:11

Day Two
Anxious for Nothing

Be anxious for nothing, but in everything by prayer and supplication, with thanksgiving, let your requests be made known to God; and the peace of God, which surpasses all understanding, will guard your hearts and minds through Christ Jesus.
~ Philippians 4:6-7

Wow. Now there's a promise.

It's hard to imagine being anxious for nothing, isn't it? Worry and anxiety play a part in all our lives to some degree. They rob us of fully embracing life, and can steal away our joy and contentment. Anxiety and worry, like almost all negative emotions, are driven by fear. In Matthew 6:25 Jesus tells us not to worry about our life. He points out that it's pointless and of no value because of our security and provision in God.

The definition of this word *worry* in the Greek language states: "to be anxious about, take thought; from a root word that means to disunite, divide, be different from through distraction, care, concern." Interesting. When we worry, we become distracted and concerned, but have you ever thought you were disunited? Think about it. When we worry, fear takes the place of our faith and we begin to disunite from our connection with God. There is interference in the link between us.

Isn't it interesting how we learned yesterday that the Greek word for peace means "to join?" Here we see worry, one of the opposites of peace, that means to *disunite*. Our peace depends on our unity with God, and our unity with God depends on our ability to dispel fear and worry with faith. When Adam and Eve ate the forbidden fruit, they experienced fear and worry for the first time. They disobeyed and broke the unity they had with God and immediately started to be anxious about their nakedness, fussing about how to cover themselves. When they heard God coming, they hid. First time for that too.

God called to them saying, "Where are you?" (As if He didn't know.) Adam replied, "I heard your voice and I was afraid." Up to this point we find no evidence of fear or anxiety with Adam or Eve. Once they sinned, fear stepped in as a result of their separation from God and you probably know the rest of the story.

So it goes to say that fear, worry, and anxiety separate us from the outpouring of God's power and his attributes, including his grace. Fear has always been in competition with our faith, even in the beginning. Satan tempted Eve with the fear of missing out on something better, which prompted her to momentarily abandon her faith in God's advice and provision and take the route of disobedience.

Fear and worry separate us from grace and truth. Faith brings connection, peace, and grace (divine influence) through the Holy Spirit. Philippians 4: 6-7 (above) gives us great instruction on how to replace fear and worry with faith. Here's the plan:

- Pray about anything and everything.
- Let God know the requests of your heart.
- Thank him for who he is, what he has done, and what he is able to do.

- Keep your mind focused on *truth*.
- Don't allow imaginations or presumptions to occupy your thoughts.

The verse that follows finalizes the instruction: "Finally, brethren, whatever things are true, whatever things are noble, whatever things are just, whatever things are pure, whatever things are lovely, whatever things are of good report, if there is any virtue and if there is anything praiseworthy-meditate on these things" (Philippians 4:8).

The reward? The peace of God that exceeds all understanding will be with you guarding your heart.

Today's Peace Challenge: If you find you are anxious or worried about something, try this plan as mapped out for us in this Word from Philippians. Remember, faith is like exercise. The more we do it, the better the results. Don't be discouraged by first steps.

Further Reading: Proverbs 12:25, Psalm 94:19, Matthew 6:25-34, 2 timothy 1:7

Day Three

Swinging Bridges

My people are destroyed from lack of knowledge.
~ Hosea 4:6

Have you ever tried to walk across one of those swinging rope bridges? The kind that are suspended over a cavern or river that seems miles below?

They are very frightening to me. I don't like heights at all. Add any movement to the mix, and I am in instant panic. All I have to do is step one foot on the bridge and it begins to move and sway. Each step I take intensifies the movement and my fear. By the time I'm in the middle, trying not to look or think of the devastating drop beneath me, my mind isn't even spitting out one rational thought. I'm invaded with visions of disaster and thoughts of horror. Yikes!

Let's back up and try this again. Suppose that before I cross that bridge, I do some research. I learn about the person who designed the bridge and how it was constructed. I research the integrity of its design and strength, the thickness of the ropes and the strength of what they are anchored to. After getting in touch with the designer, we develop a relationship and I grow to trust his wisdom and ability to create a strong and safe structure that allows people to cross the bridge safely. Knowing him, I am assured his personal character is trustworthy. I become confident he would never design a bridge that would fail and cause disaster. He even offers to cross the bridge with me.

Now I can cross the bridge. My fear is gone because I now trust the builder and the bridge. Even though the bridge is still swaying and the water is swirling below me, the height doesn't overwhelm me and the movement seems less threatening because I am enjoying the view and the experience.

So it is with the peace that God offers us. 2 Peter 1:2 says, "Grace and peace be multiplied to you *in the knowledge of God* and of Jesus our Lord," (italics mine). The verse in Hosea at the top of the devotion declares that we can be destroyed by our lack of knowledge concerning God. These words give us insight as to how to obtain peace. They convey the message, it is by knowing God that we gain peace.

Just like any relationship, we have to really get to know someone before we can trust them and feel peaceful and at ease in their presence. Through our knowledge and familiarity with God, we can find an oasis of peace during difficult times and difficult Christmases. We can find strength to face that holiday gathering we're dreading. We can walk through empty days swallowed up by grief over the loss or absence of a loved one, knowing we can count on God's presence and comfort being with us.

God doesn't necessarily smooth out the road (or keep the bridge from swaying), but he will provide what we need to get through it. Our part is to get to know him and then rely on him. He reveals himself through the words of the Bible, through the magnificence of nature, through other believers, and through our stillness as we take time to listen for him. We must *choose* to take time and be diligent to know and understand him. As we do, he reveals more and more of himself to us and lavishes us with his benefits and attributes. We can't expect to have God's peace in times of distress if we have made no effort to get to know him.

Allow time this week, this season, and in the days to come to diligently pursue discovering more about God and who he is. May his peace be multiplied to you as your understanding increases. He is our peace.

Today's Peace Challenge: Choose an aspect of God's character to focus on today. It could be his love, faithfulness, creativity, power, or kindness. If you have time, use a concordance to do a word search on the characteristic you have chosen, revealing how God exhibits that characteristic. Ask God to reveal that characteristic to you as you go through your day. You may see it in someone's kindness, some good news, a sunset, a verse of scripture, or a million other things. Watch closely.

Repeat this exercise often and you will grow in your knowledge of God.

Further Reading: Psalm 9:10, Psalm 46:10, Ephesians 3: 17-19, 2 Peter 1:2-4

Day Four
Perspective

"A particular attitude toward or way of regarding something. A point of view."
~ Taken from: Google Dictionary

The Christmas season can press us into places and situations that we would rather not be in or downright dread. It could be an office party or family gathering where you feel out of place, share different lifestyles or values, or feel frustration with certain personalities or demeanor.

Maybe it's the stress of finagling your way through noisy, crowded stores or bumper-to-bumper traffic. Perhaps your finances are screaming "Stop!" and the pressures to buy are shouting, "But it's Christmas!" The temptations of comparing, perfecting, lamenting, and dreading are pushing you dangerously close to a Christmas cliff.

So how do we manage these unfavorable and difficult situations?

Perspective can make all the difference. We all have the ability to choose our perspective. The way we view or perceive a situation is entirely our choice, and it will form our response. Our perspective can determine the outcome and it will certainly determine the way it affects us.

Consider Mark 10:13-15. Jesus had been teaching multitudes of people who had gathered to listen. The Pharisees in the crowd were harassing him with questions to test him. I'm sure Jesus was physically tired and, most likely, weary of the provoking questions. People began bringing children to Jesus to be blessed. The disciples saw this as an intrusion and scolded those who brought them. Jesus saw it as an opportunity and encouraged the children to come to him, and he blessed them. The blessing of the children was released by Jesus' perspective, but would have been blocked by the perspective of the disciples. Likewise, our perspective in times of unfavorable situations can either release God's power or block it.

Difficult situations can give us opportunity to be God's conduit for love, peace, or comfort to come into play. However, we need to release our hold on a negative view, and shift our thinking toward a God view, in order for God to be released to work through us. When things seem too overwhelming, or beyond our ability, it gives God opportunity to show his power and compassion to us; however, we won't be able to receive it if our perspective is negative.

So, how do we maintain a proper perspective? Colossians 3:2 tells us, "Set your mind on things above, not on things of the earth." We tend to get stuck on the issue, annoyance, or limitation and our mind becomes set. It's like a computer screen in our head freezes and won't let us "click out." All our efforts to eliminate our ruminating and stressing over the issue seem ineffective.

Our only recourse is to replace the negative thoughts with a new and different thought: to renew it. We need to set our mind only on truth because God himself is truth. Truth comes *from* God, and truth sets us free. Staying focused on positive aspects and on the truth of God's ability to influence the situation, brings us into a position to receive that influence. God can then provide what we need to get through the situation, and his will can be accomplished. Romans 12:2 confirms this: "Be transformed by the renewing of your mind, that you may prove what is that good and acceptable and perfect will of God."

Transformed. Pretty grandiose word. It can happen though. Our perspective does transform. To renew something is to put effort into bringing something back to its originally intended purpose or condition. To do that, we have to be aware of its original intension or design. This often requires being in touch with the designer. Herein lies the key to achieving a new perspective. We need to rely on our designer: God, who knows us, desires unity and relationship with us, and created us in his image.

This is his originally intended purpose for us. His image is love, truth, mercy, power, and goodness. He can fill us with these same attributes if we ask for them and seek them. That is grace. Remember, one of the meanings for grace is, "The divine influence upon the heart, and its reflection in the life." If we seek God's divine influence on our perspective and the situation, transformation can occur. God is eager to, "show the exceeding riches of His grace in His kindness toward us in Christ Jesus." (Ephesians 2:7.) We just need to reach out for it in faith to release his power and influence.

In order to achieve a godly perspective, we also need to search out the truth in the situation. Too often, our negative perspective is based on lies or assumptions that have no basis of truth. Let's go back to Jesus and the children. The disciples most likely assumed that Jesus was tired, and that the children would frustrate him, but that wasn't the truth. Jesus wanted the children to come to him. Even if he was tired, the truth is that God could sustain him, and did, to be able to receive the children and bless them.

Too often, our automatic human response to difficulty is to gravitate to the negative and bypass truth. If I were to receive news that I had just been fired from my job, I would have two perspectives to choose from.

- Even though none of these thoughts are based on truth but are merely assumptions, I could become distraught and entertain thoughts of never finding another job, losing my home and reputation, and a lost or suffering career.

- Or I can diligently stay focused only on truth such as: My future is uncertain but I am breathing. New opportunities could come of this. God can provide. My skills and abilities are valuable. I have love and support from others. God will see me through this.

Thoughts that rely on God are based on truth because he *is* truth. Speaking out promises from Scripture and personalizing them can also keep us focused on truth such as, God has not given me a spirit of fear, but of power and of love and of a sound mind. (From 2 Timothy 1:7) Or, God will not leave me or forsake me. (From Hebrews 13:5)

So this Christmas season, whatever you are facing, whatever might be testing your patience or stealing your peace, whatever you might even be dreading, depend on God's divine influence. That influence can release his power, peace, wisdom, or whatever might be needed to bring transformation. It may not mean that things will change, but your heart will. He is God with us—Immanuel. We are not alone and we don't have to do life alone. His influence brings truth and transformation as we keep our minds set on him.

Today's Peace Challenge: Practice setting your mind on truth if you find your mind wandering into the negative zone. Choose the healthy perspective and allow God to work in and through you. When he does be ready to record and share your experience.

Further Reading: Psalm 84:11-12, John 1:14-17, Acts 4:33, 2 Corinthians 12:9, 2 Corinthians 13:14

Day Five

Contentment

I have learned in whatever state I am, to be content.
~ Philippians 4:11

We all have needs and desires. It is also our human condition and intrinsic nature to want *more*. It was the motivating factor behind the original sin. Adam and Eve were not content with what God had given them and just wanted "one more thing." The temptation to have something they didn't already have was just too great.

Discontent and longing for more can lead us to a place of depression, burnout, conflict, indebtedness, and general unhappiness. We live in a broken, imperfect world and we all deal with imperfect bodies, relationships, and circumstances. How we deal with that imperfection determines the quality of contentment we will experience.

How do we get to that place of contentment? What can we do to maintain a sense of peace and be free of that restless feeling of discontent in an imperfect world? More specifically, how do we remain in that state during the Christmas season that screams the demand of *more*?

- More presents to buy. (Is what I bought enough?)
- More decorations. (Look what the neighbors put up.)

- More cookies to bake. (Should I take some to the office and maybe the nursing home?)
- More Christmas cards to send. (Susie sent me one last year and I didn't send one to her.)
- One more gift for Tommy or he might notice Joey got more.
- And certainly more money to facilitate all of the above.

I think our first step away from all this craziness is to truly identify need. According to Strong's Concordance, the definition of *need* from its Greek origin means, "requirement or destitution, lack, necessity." With this in mind, let's sort out the difference between *need* and *desire*.

Desire is the strong feeling of wanting something or wishing for something. The Greek and Hebrew definitions use the words, "crave" and "longing." I think it is safe to say that a need requires a resource that would stabilize our very existence. A desire is a feeling of wanting more than what we have. We *need* provision, health, and shelter. We *desire* an enticing meal, a lovely complexion, and a beautiful home.

The way our society celebrates Christmas can set us up for discontent or feelings of inadequacy. Perhaps you are fantasizing of a lovely decorated home, dozens of yummy Christmas treats, the family gathered around a well-endowed, beautifully dressed table, and everyone getting along in sweet harmony—a perfect, picture-postcard Christmas.

Realistically, most of us don't experience the postcard Christmas, or even come close. Too many of us sacrifice our peace and sanity trying to create it. It's possible this fantasy will not become reality for you because of broken relationships, financial challenges, loss of a loved one, separation or distance, or any number of extenuating circumstances. Perhaps some of you come close to the postcard Christmas, but it takes everything out of you to get there, and you may still struggle with elements of discontent.

I believe our greatest solution to avoid depression, burnout, or discontent during these days of Christmas preparation, as well as any time of the year, is acceptance with faith. I don't mean resignation. Resignation, as defined by Dictionary.com, means, "an accepting, unresisting attitude ... submission." That carries with it an attitude of defeat. I'm talking about acceptance of the reality of what is lacking, with an attitude of faith for provision and a heart of thankfulness for what exists.

In the 13th chapter of Numbers we read where Moses sent spies into the Promised Land to check it out. There were twelve men who went. Ten of them returned with negative reports, focusing only on the frightening size and number of the inhabitants—not on the abundance of provision they saw in the land that was "flowing with milk and honey."

Joshua and Caleb were the only two men who returned with positive reports. They expressed their belief in the fact that they would be able to overcome the giants in the land with God's help. They conveyed the abundance and goodness they had seen and expressed their confidence in God's ability to overcome where their own strength was lacking, encouraging the congregation to turn from their fear and trust God. The people, however, wanted something better, something easier, which inevitably caused them to wander in the wilderness for forty years and miss out on the goodness that God had planned for them.

God had given King David many blessings: power, wealth, victory, and peace to name a few. King David's desire for *more* when he took Bathsheba for his pleasure, caused his life to spiral into loss and pain from the consequences of that untamed desire.

How many of us miss what God intends for us because we get ahead of the game and want that new thing, or our desire for more takes over? How many times have we missed enjoying what we have, because we are too eager to attain something that seems better? How often do we run from things that seem too hard and search for the easy way, forgetting that God can give us what we need to overcome? There are so many great blessings in the simple pleasures and provisions that are part of our *now*. An attitude of thankfulness for what we have, courage to be our best, and faith in God to provide what we lack, is the best recipe for contentment.

Most of us have heard The Serenity Prayer by Reinhold Niebuhr: "God grant me the serenity to accept the things I cannot change, the courage to change the things I can, and the wisdom to know the difference." It is great wisdom to follow, but let's take a look at the rest of that prayer that isn't as commonly recited.

> "Living one day at a time, enjoying one moment at a time, accepting hardships as the pathway to peace. Taking, as He did, this sinful world as it is (acceptance), not as I would have it (don't force the fantasy); trusting that He will make all things right if I surrender to His will; that I may be reasonably happy (no promise of a rose garden) in this life and supremely happy in the next." (Parentheses mine.)

There you have it, a plan to follow for contentment and serenity. Ecclesiastes 4:6 (NIV) reminds us, "Better one handful with tranquility than two handfuls with toil and chasing after the wind."

If you find yourself chasing after the wind this season or wandering in a wilderness of depression, debt, or discontent, look for the things in your life that you can be thankful for. Fully enjoy those things. Rest in the ability of God to provide what is lacking and give you courage to accept what is not in your power to change. Allow this Christmas to be a time when you bask in the blessings of God's faithfulness and provision.

Today's Peace Challenge: Open your eyes and your heart to the blessings you have. List them, enjoy and embrace them, and employ thankfulness.

Further Reading: Habakkuk 3:17-19, Proverbs 15:16-17, Proverbs 23:4-5, Matthew 6:33-34, Matthew 6:19-20, Philippians 4: 10-13, I Timothy 6:6

Day Six

Loneliness

A great fire burns within me, but no one stops to warm
themselves by it, and passersby only see a wisp of smoke.
~ Vincent Van Gogh

It seems that loneliness is never fully satisfied. It is always with us to some extent. Oh yes, we have encounters of distraction from it—possibly even momentary satiety—in fellowship, comradery, and moments of intimacy. But even in those times, aren't we desiring to know that person on an even deeper level and longing to be more fully known by them? Our humanity is always craving love and validation in the depths of who we are.

I feel it. Loneliness never fully leaves. Like hunger, it is only temporarily satisfied and returns perpetually. Its intensity and overwhelming heaviness in times of solidarity, and the empty, hollow, gnawing, sadness of being alone, keeps coming back to taunt me. I have felt it in a crowded room of familiar friends. It can surface as I sit at a table with a dozen family members or in the company of a close friend. Its presence was felt in my marriage and now in my singleness. I have felt it in the absence of one dearly loved, and I've felt it in their presence as well.

If it never fully leaves us, and is never fully satisfied, it seems we have been created this way intentionally. It is in all of us. This empty longing craves fulfillment and drives us to pursue that fulfillment. It is the motivation and driving force behind our pursuit of all things. We pursue love, friendship, sex, power, money, and material things—all those and more—in hopes of satisfying the longing, the craving. We are looking to be fully validated, fully known, and fully loved. We search for ways to eradicate the dreaded emptiness that plays a taunting game with our sense of value and self-esteem. It is a monster that can lure our hearts to fall prey to temptations that masquerade as satisfaction or fulfillment.

We must conclude that this is a void which can never be fully filled. It is a part of us that we cannot change. To be content with it, we must accept it and find a way to be at peace. It is as much an inevitable part of us as our hunger for food.

In as much as we must work, hunt, and gather to satisfy our empty stomachs; so must we engage in similar effort to stave off the pangs of loneliness. We cannot sit back and expect relationships to happen without some pursuit on our part, investing our time and participation.

Yet, in our pursuit, we cannot demand or expect another to fill the void. We cannot hold too tightly or we will squeeze the life and freedom out of any interaction. We must fully embrace and delight in the temporary pleasure and bliss of companionship, comradery, and intimacy when it occurs, but be willing to let it go with a peaceful and grateful heart when time releases it. In its absence we must realize and accept that no one can remain deep enough within us, or long enough with us, except one: God. He created that longing and void in us to be filled and satisfied by and through our relationship with him. We cannot successfully satisfy it with the temporal aspects of humanity alone. Loneliness has a spiritual element, and the human spirit cannot reach its depths.

It is through our communion with God's Spirit that we find a sense of peace and ease from the longing. Even then, we long to know more of God since our human minds cannot fully penetrate the depth of who he is. However, unlike any human presence, he is unchanging, solid, trustworthy, and always there. He does not leave or betray us, nor does he forget. He created us to long for him, to pursue him continually, and promises we will find him in that pursuit.

There is no end to our longing, not in this life. If there were, we would find ourselves with no need of God. He created us to desire him. He desires us. We are created in his image with the same longings. We fulfill each other. God delights in us and loves us. We are not alone.

"The only time we waste is the time we
spend thinking we are alone."
~ Mitch Albom

"All great and precious things are lonely."
~ John Steinbeck

"Solitude is fine but you need someone to tell solitude is fine."
~ Honore' de Belzac

(above quotes from goodreads.com)

Today's Peace Challenge: If you are struggling with loneliness, consider being proactive to find some diversion. Interact with people. Look for a group to join that expresses your interests. Look for opportunities to do some volunteer work. Invite a friend or a neighbor for coffee or to do lunch. If loneliness isn't a struggle for you right now, think of someone who might be lonely. A phone call or an invitation from you might perk them up. Strive to become more aware of others in your life that might be lonely. Pursue a deeper relationship with God using the same steps you would take in any other relationship. Learn more about him. Converse with him. Tune your thoughts to be aware of his influence and presence in your world.

Further Reading: Isaiah 58:9, Psalm 73:23-24, Psalm 139, John 14:18, Romans 8:38-39

Day Seven
O Come, O come, Immanuel, and Ransom Captive Israel

Yes. We are captives. Captives of commercialism and society's expectations of us during this season of Christmas. A season that celebrates the most profound gift of freedom from captivity possible. How ironic. A season that should bring us to a quiet, simple Sabbath of peaceful reflection and humble gratitude. Oh how we have lost it's meaning in the chaos.

For years during the weeks leading up to Christmas, I found myself leaping out of bed in the mornings and skipping my normal quiet time with God. There was just too much on my to-do list. I was overwhelmed with all the things I needed to accomplish to be ready for the Big Day. Wow. Skipping my time with the Lord because of Christmas? What's up with that? It wasn't right, and I knew it, but the momentum of the frenzy had me in its grip.

Helping at school parties, shopping for gift lists a mile long, baking goodies, cards to write and send, packages to wrap, decorations to be finished, planning food and get-togethers, school concerts, church activities ... *Aye yai yai.* Giving up my quiet time? Really? That's worse than giving up a relaxing bath for a cold shower or looking forward to a romantic dinner out and slaving over a hot stove instead.

This season commemorates the birth and gift of our Lord and Savior who gave his life for us and lived among us to allow us to know him and God the Father. He woos us and longs for us to have a relationship with him. In return, he promises us so much; peace, strength, joy, and hope. Yet in his time of honor and recognition, we can find ourselves casting our time with him aside for superficial things.

In my opinion, the perfect way to celebrate Christmas would be for everything to stop for a few days. Activities and work would pause, and we would empty our schedules instead of adding to them. Our only expectations would be to create an oasis of serenity and undisturbed time for grateful reflection, prayer, worship, and focused celebration of who Christ is in our lives and what he has done for us. When we celebrate the birthday of a loved one, don't we pour out all our time and attention on them? How poorly we miss the mark for the birthday of Jesus.

Lord Jesus, come, you who are God with us. Ransom us from the captivity of expectations and chaos we put on ourselves and others. Humble us to allow you to lead us to a place of peace and simplicity in our celebration of you.

Today's Peace Challenge: Spend time in prayer and reflection concerning the activities around your traditions and celebrations of Christmas. Are there places where change needs to take place? If so, take one step toward that change. Don't be too hard on yourself. Remember, you can only eat an elephant one bite at a time.

Further Reading: Isaiah 61:1, Matthew 13:18-23, Luke 10:38-42, John 6:26-27, John 15:1-13, 2 Corinthians 4:18

Week Three

JOY

Day One
The Pursuit of Happiness

In Your presence is fullness of joy.
~ Psalm 16:11

Today we light the third Advent candle that signifies Joy.

Happiness. We all want it. We all make choices in hopes of attaining it. We are content when we achieve it and lament when it is absent. We spend the majority of our time doing any number of things to obtain it, yet we have absolutely no control over it. It can slip away as quickly as a single moment. A meanly spoken word, bad news, a challenging or disappointing incident, or any number of things can steal it away from us very quickly. Happiness is fleeting and fickle and is totally reliant on circumstances or our own meager efforts.

Joy, however, is different. It is more enduring and stable and is not a result of our effort or dictated by our circumstances. True joy is a gift passed on to us by God himself. It is an attribute of the essence of his divine character; a gift from his Spirit as recorded in Galatians 5:22. This gift of joy is something we receive by believing and pursuing God. When we remain in touch with him, we are recipients of this joy that can become enduring in any circumstance. It's not the jumping around, "I'm so excited!" feeling that happiness brings. It is a deep satisfying assurance of love, acceptance, and trust. It dispels fear and establishes a sense of safety, contentment, and expectancy. It really is very hard to describe. In fact, 1 Peter 1:8 describes it as, "Joy inexpressible and full of glory." Indeed it is. It is full of glory from God himself and it is impossible to find words to fully describe it.

Thankfully, we don't have to jump through any hoops or spend a lifetime pursuing joy to experience it. It is a gift from God's Spirit to ours when our spirit is in tune with and enmeshed with his. Remarkably, it is not the only gift from his Holy Spirit. Love, peace, patience, kindness, goodness, faithfulness, gentleness, and self-control are a few of the effects of being focused on God, which keeps his Spirit active and alive in us. Such amazing and benevolent gifts. Such amazing grace.

In our own human effort, we often try desperately to obtain and impart these characteristics in our daily lives and interactions, and all too often we come up short. The fabric of our humanity with its impulses, cravings, and demands of gratification are powerful. They employ themselves effortlessly against our resolve to be or do better in these areas. Galatians 5:17 tells us, "For the flesh lusts against the Spirit and the Spirit against the flesh; and these are contrary to one another, so that you do not do the things that you wish."

So there we have it. The word *lust* in this verse means, "a longing (especially for what is forbidden) - desire." Our humanity has a strong desire against the Spirit, so therein lies our struggle. We can no more fight our humanity with our humanity than we can fight fire with fire. However, this verse also reminds us that the Holy Spirit has a strong desire against our humanity's depravity. Therein lies our hope and our defense. "I say then; Walk in the Spirit and you shall not fulfill the lust of the flesh" (Galatians 5:16).

How do we walk in the Spirit? It's much the same as walking through life with anyone we love. We seek their presence, make time for them, and give them our full attention. We give them our trust and confide in them. We tune our awareness to them, listen to them, and remain willing for them to open their heart to us. We praise them and validate and acknowledge their love for us and their benevolence toward us. Walking in the Spirit is the continual pursuit and experience of a love relationship with God.

As we embark on this third week of advent with its celebration of joy, may we exercise these elements of a love relationship in our walk with God. Let's open our hearts to him, make time for him, and allow his Spirit to mesh with ours. Let's intentionally walk with him through these next couple weeks and beyond and let his joy spill over into our hearts and our circumstances. That joy will increase our strength to get through any bumps in the Christmas road because, "Do not sorrow for the joy of the LORD is your strength" (Nehemiah 8:10).

This Week's Joy Challenge: Take the challenge above to walk more closely with God. Create time in your schedule to spend moments of quiet with him. Read his Word. Talk to him about your day, your concerns, and your victories. See if your Joy Barometer doesn't go up. Record your joy moments or times when you sense his presence. Share them with your family, a friend, or loved one. These weekly and daily challenges can be a source of shared spiritual activity that can create bonds and a means for experiencing the blessings of God together.

Further Reading: Psalm 16:11, John 15:9-13, John 17:11-13, Romans 15:13,

Day Two
Sing

If I cannot fly, let me sing
~ Stephen Sondheim (goodreads.com)

Music is an expression of the heart and a language that reaches beyond the physical and into our spirit. When we sing, it expresses things in a richer way and goes to a deeper place than mere words can penetrate. "Music gives strength to the soul." (Lailah Gifty Akita, goodreads.com)

The Bible is full of encouragement to sing our praise and thankfulness to God and to make music with instruments as well. In 2 Chronicles 20, an enemy army was defeated while the people were singing and praising. Acts 16:25-26 records an experience of Paul and Silas in prison. When they began to sing, an earthquake erupted. The chains of the prisoners were loosed and the prison doors opened. King Saul was overcome by a "distressing spirit" from time to time and when David played his harp the spirit would leave him (see 1 Samuel 16:23).

We know there is power in praise. God is a lover of music, and he has endowed us with a wonderful gift in our ability to create it, express ourselves with it, and enjoy it. Music is able to ignite a myriad of emotions from tears to jubilation.

Christmas is a time when music is everywhere. There are great songs that express deep meaning and praise to Jesus and other songs that are just for fun. Even though the songs are meaningful and fun, I can tire of them well before Christmas. There have been a few years when hearing them brought pain and sadness because of the losses in my life and the disappointments involved with the holidays. I couldn't get through "Silent Night" without sobbing.

If you can relate to this, I know your pain and frustration. I can't offer you any suggestions as to how to escape the incessant rounds of "Jingle Bells" or "Rudolph,"—they are with us for the duration—but I do understand your heart. When you are hurting, it's hard to join in, or even listen, to the music of the Christmas season. However, there is great peace and healing that can be experienced from listening to and expressing yourself through music.

Several places in God's Word encourage us to bring "a sacrifice of praise" to God. A sacrifice is something that doesn't come easy. If we are asked to bring praise as a sacrifice, then we have to assume we are being asked to sing and praise God even when we don't feel like it, even when it is hard. The rewards of sacrifice are often great and in this instance, it is true as well. Psalm 22:3 tells us that God inhabits the praises of Israel (His people). This word *inhabit* means, "to sit down, to dwell, to remain." When we sing and praise God, he comes to us. His Spirit is with us. What a remedy for our sorrow and our pain.

In my own experience, the times that I least felt like singing—but did it out of my pain as a sacrifice—were times I felt the presence of God the strongest. As we sing of God's mercies, influence, power, and goodness it can lead us through and out of deep places of sorrow in our lives if we are willing to sacrifice our resistance toward doing so.

Psalm 84:5-7 talks about the "Valley of Baca" which means the valley of weeping or sorrow. It says, "Blessed is the man whose strength is in You, whose heart is set on pilgrimage. As they pass through the Valley of Baca they make it a spring; the rain covers it with pools. They go from strength to strength." The word *Baca* in this verse means "weeping" in Hebrew. Notice that this pilgrimage, or journey, is *passing through*, not camping, not staying around. They have *chosen* to rely on God for strength and are *determined* in their heart to pass through. It goes on to say that they make it a spring (it becomes a place of refreshing and nourishment), and rain covers it with pools (which means blessings are poured out). As a result, they become stronger and stronger. The power of praising God through song or words or even just listening intently to music of praise can bring us to a place of peace and strength, empowering us to get through our valleys of sorrow and lead us to springs of joy.

Today's Joy Challenge: Sing. Express praise to God. Turn on some music of adoration and praise to him. Really listen and put your heart's expression into some of the beautiful Christmas songs expressing adoration of our Lord. Let music take you to a place that refreshes and restores you.

Further Reading: 1Chronicles 16:9-13, 22-23, Psalm 59:16-17, Psalm 98-4-6, Psalm 100, Psalm 107:21-22, Psalm 116:17, Hebrews 13:15

Day Three

Extravagant Goodness

God has given us an amazingly complex and beautiful world to live in. There is so much beauty and goodness in us and around us. He didn't have to be so extravagant. He could have created the world to contain only what we needed to sustain life. Instead, he has masterfully created our earthly home with phenomenal beauty and creative wonders: sparkling waters, starry skies, flowers of intricate beauty, breathtaking scenery, animal life that is vast and amazing, and our own bodies that hold wonders we have yet to fully learn of. It is truly amazing and most definitely a testimony of God's lavish love for us.

Something I love to do—and find especially helpful if I'm having a bad day or going through a struggle—is to ask God to show me signs of his goodness throughout my day. He did that for me one morning as I set out for a brisk walk. I was hoping to find relief talking to God and sorting out the cobwebs of dread and worry in my mind concerning the coming holiday. A good walk has always been therapeutic for me and gives me one-on-one time with God.

It was a cold winter day, but the crisp, country air felt good and refreshing. The ground was blanketed in snow, and a light dusting of new snow was falling. Shortly after I left my driveway, I was startled by a doe and two little fawns that darted from the pines and onto the road in front of me. I stood there and watched as the three of them gazed at me with curiosity and uncertainty in their eyes and body language. Instinctively, the mother nudged them quickly into the woods on the opposite side of the road and they were soon out of sight. The reality of their beauty and the protective love of the mother overwhelmed me, and I was immediately reminded of the goodness of God. How amazing it is that he has given his creatures such loving instincts.

How many times he has nudged me into safer situations as well. The cobwebs in my mind eased up a bit and seemed less threatening. I sensed a shift in my perspective; feeling strengthened with the understanding that a God much stronger than I, and so amazing, can give me what I will need in any situation. I felt his presence in that moment. I was reminded of the joy found in the simplicity of things that are free for us to enjoy if we can slow down and open our minds and hearts to them.

During this time of Christmas, allow yourself the benefit of pressing in to awaken your senses to a higher awareness of the gifts of our Creator. If the usual sights and sounds of the season are pulling at the ache in your heart, then refocus. What evidence of God surrounds you ... now ... right where you are? The morning sky? The sun dancing across dew-covered terrain? A bird perched outside your window? Softly falling snow? A beautiful work of art? The sparkle in a child's eyes?

Whatever it might be, take a fresh look! A deeper look. There is wonder to be found all around us. The evidence of a Creator who loves us enough to create unimaginable, abundant, extravagant, beauty. Engulf yourself in the wonder and delightful magnificence of his gifts. Breathe deeply of his power and love and allow it to soothe and refresh you.

Today's Joy Challenge: Look for God today. Ask him to show you signs of his goodness, his extravagance, and his love. Keep your eyes open; you will see him. Make it a game with others. Write down what he shows you and share with family or a friend. Compare notes.

Further Reading: Job 36:24 – chapter 39, Psalm 104

Day Four
Here's a Thought

Thoughts are like an open ocean, they can either move
you forward within its waves, or sink you under deep
into its abyss.
~ Anthony Liccione (goodreads.com)

Once in a while I struggle with times of depression. During these times I wake up in the morning with a heavy spirit and an oppressive gloom overwhelming me. Sometimes a wave of emptiness or apathy will hit me at random times during my day. Frightening or discouraging thoughts can tumble into my head out of nowhere and knock my peace off balance. I can spend hours and even days in a thick fog of gloom, and my mind has no energy to find an antidote. My thoughts become crippling enemies of any effort toward a more positive outlook. I can find myself wallowing in a prison of self-inflicted misery that overshadows any joy available to me.

All this is created merely by my own thinking. For some illogical reason, I remain unaware of this fact for far too long into the senseless process, duped by my own thinking.

It is certain that Christmas can present triggers, memories, conflict, disappointments, and heartache that can make us vulnerable to this conundrum of debilitating thought, more than any other time of year.

There *is* a way out and a way to prevent the slippery slope. The key is to be aware of the beginning of the slide into that dark place and fend it off before it gathers force. As we become aware, we must choose to make a conscious effort to change our thoughts.

A starting point is to analyze what is true about the thoughts we are having in regard to our situation. So much of what we dwell on is based on lies or assumptions and has no basis of truth. The truth does set us free. Free from the grip of the negative. Once we begin to sort truth from lies, we must refuse to spend any more thought on what is not complete truth. Our thinking then needs to become focused on what *is* true about our strengths, God's power and promises, who we are in Christ, and what we can and can't change. Philippians 4:8 begins by telling us we need to think on things that are true.

> "Finally, brethren, whatever things are true, whatever things are noble, whatever things are just, whatever things are pure, whatever things are lovely, whatever things are of good report, if there is any virtue and if there is anything praiseworthy- meditate on these things."

Notice also that it asks us to think of anything praiseworthy. Combating depression with thankfulness is an amazingly effective tool. The mornings that I wake up in that cloud, I start thanking God ... that I'm alive on the cusp of a new day, I had a bed to sleep in, a warm house to wake up in, and that God is with me and for me. Truth is recognized and validated, praise is given, and the power of depression and discouragement is dismantled.

I used to work at a job that I really dreaded and disliked. My attitude could easily slip into a bitter mode of "ugly." Self-pity liked to set up camp in my thoughts and zap my joy. Finally, after far too many times working this way, I started to dialogue with God saying things like: "Lord, thank you that I am healthy enough to do this work and that I have the strength and ability to do it and do it well. Thank you that I have an opportunity to be a blessing here, that I'm going to see good results from my work, and I'll be paid when I am done." It helped immensely. My attitude shifted. Verse 9 of Philippians 4 tells us that if we practice those things in verse 8, "the God of peace will be with you." That is telling us not only his peace will be with us, but his *presence* will be also. It can't get much better than that.

If we were never depressed, we would not be fully alive and human. Our experience with these down times gives us the ability to fully relish times of happiness and joy. Continual happiness would leave no reason for us to ever seek God. Some depression is natural and even necessary to bring change. However, there are many times in our lives when we can be in a very desolate place where life seems empty and our hearts are apathetic. At times like these it is beneficial to question whether our thoughts are creating some of our misery by dwelling on things or situations that have no basis of truth. It's possible we may be overly focused on ourselves and the situation. If this is the case, we can find relief by asking God to reveal truth to us while being open and expectant about what God can do. Dismantle depression and gloom with thoughts of what is true, noble, just, pure, lovely, good, virtuous, and praiseworthy.

I believe there is action needed as well. We can't just sit around and wait to feel better. In 1 Kings 19, when Elijah was depressed and ready to give up, the angel told him to "arise and eat." Basically, it was an encouragement for him to get moving and do something to strengthen himself.

Throughout God's Word, most encounters with God's healing and power came after an individual took that first step. A man's hand was healed when he stretched it forward. A woman's ailment stopped when she pressed through the crowd to touch Jesus' robe.

The water parted when the priests stepped in. Sometimes we just have to get moving and do the next thing. Even taking that step to do the ordinary, everyday things of life, even when we don't feel like it, can move us out of a funk. As you embark on the season and encounter challenges, implement these thoughts and actions and you will see your joy reignited.

Today's Joy Challenge: Be conscious today of your thoughts. What are you spending your time and energy thinking about? Analyze your thoughts for truth. Practice Philippians 4:8.

Further Reading: Psalm 139:23-24, Proverbs 3:5-6, Proverbs 23:7a, Jeremiah 6:19, Ephesians 4:23-24

Day Five

Shine

Then your light shall break forth like the morning ...
~ Isaiah 58:8

Take a moment to read Isaiah 58:6-12. It is a recipe from God that promises to bring joy to our lives. The great thing is, it brings joy to others as well. As we extend ourselves to others, our hearts become full and God is glorified. There are so many promises in this passage of Scripture. When we discover them, it's hard to imagine why we don't do a better job of reaching out. Let's look at some of these promises.

As we read through verses 6-7, we are encouraged by God to reach out to those in need. The promise in verse 8 follows declaring, "Then your light shall break forth like the morning." Doesn't that just drip with joy? Like brilliant rays of morning sunlight searing through the darkness of night, joy breaks through the murky gloom of apathy and stale, mundane living.

Verse 10 expounds on this same promise: "Then your light shall dawn in the darkness, and your darkness shall be as the noonday." The words indicate that our light will dispel the darkness of others as well as our own. God is so efficient. There is healing promised in verse 8 and God's attentiveness in verse 9. His guidance, our contentment, and renewed strength are promised in verse 11. Wow. Such rich gifts. As we take our focus off ourselves, open our eyes, and give from our heart to those around us, things change.

So what's stopping us? Insecurity? Fear? Pride? Or are we just too caught up in our own world, our own struggle, to even notice, let alone respond to the needs or pain of others? I believe for many of us we think we need to get our own ducks in a row before we can be effective at helping someone else. Take notice, though, of verse 10. It says that our light will dawn *in* the darkness and *our darkness* will be as noonday. This passage is not an example of reaching out to the afflicted from a bright place, but from a dark place. It exemplifies that even in our personal places of challenge or brokenness we can make a difference.

Are you feeling down, discouraged, lonely, or stressed? You are not alone; there are others who are struggling too. This time of year brings heartache and hopelessness to the surface for so many people. You don't have to invite the next depressed and weary stranger home for dinner (then again you might), but it's amazing what a smile or compliment will do for someone's day. Once, after showing my I.D. to a teller, she said, "There's no way you look your age." I was smiling the rest of the day.

It's not that hard to brighten someone's day. Ask the person in line behind you how their day is going. Buy someone a hot drink who has a cold job. Give your waitress/waiter an extra big tip, call a shut in, volunteer in an area of outreach. Hold the door, smile, help, and just be thoughtful. Be listening and ready to act on God's nudges. Be aware ... be watching ... be ready to give and experience joy.

Today's Joy Challenge: Be creative and see what you can do to extend love and compassion today ... and every day.

Further Reading: Deuteronomy 14:28-29, Psalm 41:1-3, Proverbs 11:24-25, Proverbs 19:17, Matthew 25:35-40, Luke 6:38

Day Six

Fun!

A merry heart does good like a medicine.
~ Proverbs 17:22

Several years ago someone posed a question to me, "What do you do for fun?" I was stunned. I must have looked at her with a blank stare, like a deer caught in the headlights. *Fun?* My mind began churning and grasping for an answer but—much to my bewilderment—I got nothing.

I don't remember my exact answer, but I'm sure it included a confession of a life lacking fun. It really made me think. The conversation stayed on my mind for days, eventually causing me to analyze my life and make some changes. At what point did I stop having fun? I realized my life was barren in the area of activities that were for pure enjoyment and leisure. I had not been taking time to do things I really enjoyed, things that recharged me and lifted my spirits.

We can get so caught up in the details and intensity of life, and seeing to the needs and desires of loved ones, that our own need for fun and recreation gets put on a shelf.

God worked diligently for six days creating the world, but on the seventh day he rested. What do you think God did on that day of rest? What did "rest" look like for God? Did he sleep all day? Lay around and watch T.V.? Catch a few rounds of golf? Maybe he took a long walk to his favorite scenic spot. Did he find a way to have some fun? Only God knows.

The Hebrew word for rest is *shabath*, a derivative of the word Sabbath. It means "to desist from exertion, cease, celebrate, put away (down), sit still." By this definition we know God stopped his work and his doing, so it begs the question, "Was he tired?" From what we know of God it doesn't seem that he was tired. Isaiah 40:28 tells us, "The Creator of the ends of the earth neither faints nor is weary." Perhaps his rest time was used for celebrating his creative work and enjoying the grand results of his labor. A celebration of life.

Having fun is certainly a way of celebrating life. Fun allows us to cease from labor and intensity and be refreshed. What activities refresh you? What's fun for you? It's different for each of us. For one it might be dancing or playing an instrument. For another, maybe a walk in the woods or a trip to the library. Some find a gathering of friends or a sports activity to be fun, or maybe just a good nap. Whatever it is, we all need fun in our lives. It restores us and gives us a sense of confidence in the goodness of being alive.

Obviously, we can't abandon our work or responsibilities, but taking a little time for fun and relaxation is necessary for our mental and physical health. It brings an element of joy to our day, and it can be a source of joy during the Christmas season too. If the holiday presents some difficult elements that you have to deal with, make some time to weave a little fun into each day. It will help you keep a better frame of mind to handle any challenges or stresses that come your way. It doesn't have to be elaborate or take a long time—just a "fun break." Do something silly, playful, or refreshing. Involve your kids, spouse, a co-worker, or friend, or just go solo. You may find yourself creating a memory, a new Christmas tradition, or possibly discovering a new hobby or talent. We need to be intentional about lightening things up and keeping the spark in life and the joy of Christmas alive.

Today's Joy Challenge: Take a "fun break" today. Be creative. Be spontaneous.

Further Reading: Ecclesiastes 3:1, Ecclesiastes 5:16-20, Proverbs 15:13 and 15, Luke 15:22-24

Day Seven
Choices

Happiness is achieved when you stop waiting for your
life to begin and start making the most of the moment
you are in.
~ Germany Kent (goodreads,com)

How many of life's precious moments do we miss because we are obsessed and distracted with the menial details of life or absorbed in the mental entanglements of regret, guilt, or fear? How many sunsets go unobserved or a child's ploy for our attention and involvement go unnoticed?

So many opportunities to engage, enjoy, experience, comfort, help, and fully live life, slip away from us like dust in the wind, never to pass our way again. Too often, we spend much of our time and energy on what appears to be urgent, which leaves little time left for the important, meaningful, enriching, experiences of life.

My favorite expression that helps remind me of this is, "Wherever you are, be all there." This moment, right now, be fully engaged in what is going on around you and who you are with. Be fully aware of the sights, the sounds, the smells, the feelings, and the atmosphere. Listen intently, watch with interest, allow yourself to be fully engaged, fully in tune, fully enchanted.

Even our darker moments can hold treasures of new understanding, enlightenment, and consolation. All this is reliant on choice. We *choose* how to spend our life, our days, and our moments within the framework of what we can control. Granted, there is much in life that is beyond our control, but we do have power over how we choose to *be* in the moments that make up our lives.

For many and various reasons, Christmas can be a hard time for some of us, but choosing to be fully aware and fully engaged in the experience of each moment can escalate our joy and our pleasure. Implementing this choice helps us find meaning in each moment by freeing us from focusing on negative thoughts and emotions.

I am not advocating living in a state of false bliss and denial. There are plenty of necessary solitary and reflective moments in life to sort through our mental and emotional struggles in order to find healing and resolution. There are also times when it may be wise to disengage or remove ourselves from situations that are unhealthy or detrimental to our peace or safety. Being fully present in the moment can help us with these choices as well, and help us discern when we need to disengage.

Christmas is a time to celebrate hope, love, and life. I truly believe we need to engage in activities during the season that help us celebrate those things in a simple fashion and in a way that we can be "all there." Because I spent too many days preceding Christmas stressed out and weighed down with dread and gloom, I lost a lot of precious moments and days during those times. My head was so full of my own struggle with things that it left little room for awareness and enjoyment or even the pursuit of alternate ways to celebrate and honor the meaning of Christmas.

The loss can be great. Eventually, I realized this. I also became aware that my attitude was not honoring what God did for us through Jesus' birth. I began to make choices that helped me "seize the day" and stay "in the moment" in order to experience the hope, peace, joy, and love that Christmas can hold. As far as I was able, I said, "No" to all things that made me feel very sad, fearful, or upset. The things that weren't viable options to eliminate or say "No" to, I purposed to be fully engaged in any element of it that was good and would help me keep my peace. I'm still learning and developing ways to implement this practice so that, wherever I am during this season, I can be all there. This gives me an advantage to experience the joy God has for all of us in these Christmas moments.

Today's Joy Challenge: Practice being "all there" in whatever you do today. Seize the Day. It won't come again.

Further Reading: Ephesians 5:15-16, James 4:13-17, Psalm 90:10-17

Week Four

LOVE

Day One
Love Letters

Behold what manner of love the Father has bestowed
on us that we should be called children of God.
~ 1 John 3:1

The fourth and last candle of the Advent wreath is lit today, signifying God's love for us.

I love the Scripture above. It speaks so warmly of the personal, relational and caring love of God. God's love is the deep, unconditional love of a father. This is what we are celebrating at Christmas. The love God has for us was communicated in an amazing way by sending his son, his likeness, into our world. God placed Jesus here to walk among us so we would come to know him and experience his power and his love. By sending Jesus, God gave mankind the opportunity to know things about himself experientially.

In John 12:45 Jesus says, "He who sees me sees Him who sent me." Jesus, sent by God, who had God in him, and who was in God, and who was God, walked among men and women like you and me. They hung out with him, ate with him, worked with him, laughed and cried with him. They were amazed by him, healed by him, and learned from him. He showed them God.

Jesus settled forever the breakup of mankind's unity with God that was created by the disobedience and unbelief of Adam and Eve. Jesus reversed it by his own obedience to become the final sacrifice for sin. He reversed what man did in the Garden on all points. He made it possible to be reunited in relationship with God as we believe, express our need of him, and acknowledge our falling short of God's standard in the conduct of our lives. What an amazing sacrifice God made so that we would have direct communion and interaction with him. He wants a love relationship with us.

We all desire love and are created to need love. Christmas is a time full of messages, songs, and visuals of love. If love is lacking in our lives, it can be a very difficult time. That lack becomes more pronounced with all the additional emphasis on love. Christmas isn't about earthly love though; it's about a love that is eternal, faithful, and always, always, available. Listen to the love in these words of Jesus as he is talking to his Father. First, he prays for his disciples and then he prays, "I do not pray for these alone, but for those who will believe in Me through their word; that they all may be one as You, Father are in Me, and I in You; that they also may be one in Us, that the world may believe that You sent me. And the glory which You gave Me I have given them, that they may be one just as We are one: I in them, and You in Me; that they may be made perfect in one, and that the world may know that You have sent Me, and have loved them as You have loved Me." (John 17: 20-23).

What an extravagantly beautiful expression of God's love. He desperately wants us to love him, so much so that he gave his Son over to a horrible death for us. It is definitely a love worth exploring and knowing.

If our heart is aching and crying out for love, if our desire is to be more loving, or if we really want to know God's love in a deeper way, God is able to fulfill those desires from his very nature of love. Our part is to reach out to him and take the time to get to really know him. How? Just talk to him like you would a friend. Read his Word. Reflect on it and seek deeper understanding. In the Scripture of John 17 above, notice Jesus' words, "those who will believe in Me through their word." The words written by his disciples and other followers are there for us to get to know God's heart and the heart of his son Jesus.

In this last week of advent, bathe your heart and soul with his words given to us and kept for us down through the ages. Let them sink into every fiber of your being and any places that hurt. As you read the devotions ahead for this week, take each Love Challenge and see if God's love doesn't overwhelm you.

This Week's Love Challenge: Spend time in God's Word every day, even if it's only a verse or two. Talk to God and share your heart with him. Ask him to show you his love and to cause your love to grow for others.

Further Reading: Jeremiah 31:3, Zephaniah 3:17, John 15:9-17, 1 Corinthians 2:9, Ephesians 2:4-7, 1 John 4:16

Day Two

Unloved

We all desire to be loved. It is innate in all of us. It is our greatest need. To feel unloved or rejected is undoubtedly one of the greatest wounds we can receive. It cuts to a depth so intense that we can find no way to swiftly ease its wrenching agony or turn from it. Its consuming weight and pain on our heart and soul leaves no room for other feelings, engulfing them in their attempt to surface. It strips us of confidence and self-worth. The pain is magnified according to the intensity of our own expectations of love and acceptance from the one who has wounded or betrayed us.

We have all experienced these feelings on some level, at one time or another. No one goes through life unscathed, simply because of the self-absorbed, frequently unkind nature of mankind. Even Jesus felt rejection.

Christmas is a time when family and friends gather. Plans are made, invitations sent, preparations begin, miles are traveled, and love is exchanged. These experiences warm our heart and bring contentment and joy.

But there are those who may not have been included in any holiday festivities. Invitations never came. Maybe distance separates them from loved ones or unresolved conflicts have caused rejection or fear. Possibly, the loss of someone dearly loved has left them very alone or feeling out of place. Perhaps health issues, disability, or lack of provision has left them isolated. In these cases, the Christmas season can loom ahead empty and foreboding. These people may find themselves mere bystanders, watching as the rest of the world is included in the festivities and exchanges of love. If this is where you find yourself this season, you are most assuredly not alone and there is comfort available.

God created us with an intense desire to be loved, knowing full well the tendencies of mankind toward unkindness, judgement, and self-absorbed depravity. Thankfully, he does not leave us without means to fulfill that desire. God himself is love. His very make up and character is love expressed. 1 John 4:8 and verse 16 say, "God is love." God cannot be separated from love nor can true love exist without God.

"Beloved let us love one another for love is of God; and everyone who loves is born of God and knows God. He who does not love does not know God, for God is love" (1 John 4:7-8). The love that embodies God, which is spoken of in that passage, is *agape* love. This kind of love is defined as: "an undefeatable generosity and unconquerable goodwill that always seeks the highest good of the other person. It is a self-giving love that gives freely without asking for anything in return. It does not consider the worth of its object." (Word Wealth, *love*, The Spirit Filled Life Bible). Now exchange that definition of agape, with the word love in the above verse in 1 John.

Wow. That is the kind of love I'm looking for, how about you? Does it exist in the places we tend to look for it? Doubtful. This explains our unquenched and disappointed desire for love and why we may find ourselves in a place of feeling rejected and unloved. Humanity, without the empowerment of God's love in us, isn't even close to being capable of that kind of love. Even with the empowerment of God's love within us, we are still at risk of

85

being overcome by our weakness and human resistance to God's Spirit. Agape love is a love by *choice* and an act of the will, not a consequence of emotion.

"No love of the natural heart is safe unless the human heart has been satisfied by God first."(My Utmost For His Highest, Oswald Chambers). These words of Oswald Chambers speak the undeniable truth that human love is not safe. Human love fails us, disappoints us, and rejects us at times. It is *not* always safe. God's love *is* safe. It is safe because it is perfect, true, and unfailing. It is agape. "There is no fear in love (agape) but perfect love (agape) casts out fear." 1 John 4:18 (parentheses mine).

God's love never runs out and he is never overwhelmed or put off by our constant need of it. He doesn't allow us to be consumed by our lack or by our pain if we look to him.

"Through the LORD'S mercies we are not consumed because His compassions fail not. They are new every morning. Great is Your faithfulness. The LORD is my portion, says my soul, therefore I hope in Him" (Lamentations 3:22-24).

Yes. The Lord is our portion (our fulfillment). He alone is the provider of unfailing love. We need to lean into him and allow ourselves to be loved by him, to abide (stay, remain, be present) in him and with him.

"As the Father loved Me, I also have loved you, abide in My love" (John 15:9).

Today's Love Challenge: Choose one of the verses below or from today's reading and memorize it or write it on a notecard. Repeat it over and over to yourself throughout the day. Keep God close in your thoughts. Ask him to assure you of his love for you.

Further Reading: Psalm 9:9-10, Psalm 10:14, Psalm 23, Psalm 27:10, Psalm 36:5-9, Psalm 41:7-13, Psalm 91, Psalm 94:14, Psalm 121, Isaiah 54:5-8

Day Three
The Love Circle

*In as much as you did it to one of the least of these My
brethren, you did it to Me.*
~ Matthew 25:40b

God's love is there for us ... always, but as in any relationship,
we must choose to remain closely connected to him to receive it.
Purposeful connection to him and the adherence to the things he
asks of us in his Word keep us in a position to experience his love.
It also keeps us in position to be endowed with other aspects
of his character and Spirit as well such as, joy, peace, patience,
kindness, goodness, faithfulness, gentleness, and self-control to
name a few.

When Jesus was asked by his disciples which commandment
was the greatest, he answered, "You shall love the LORD your God
with all your heart, with all your soul, and with all your mind. This
is the first and great commandment. And the second is like it: You
shall love your neighbor as yourself" (Matthew 22:37-39).

I find it interesting that Jesus said the second commandment
is like the first. It reiterates what is said in Matthew 25:40 above.
When we love and do for others, it's the same as doing it for God. As
we reach out to others in love—as God has asked us to—it creates

a circle of love. We love God and receive love from God; we then give love to others, God receives love from our giving, and he then pours love back to us. We receive a double blessing of love, not only by receiving from God, but many times from those we have blessed. It's a beautiful thing and a win-win for all.

God has given each of us certain giftings, talents, provision, knowledge, and wisdom. He has blessed us in specific ways, not just for our own benefit, but for the purpose of sharing those gifts and expanding the extent of his love in the world. "As each one has received a gift, minister it to one another, as good stewards of the manifold grace of God" (1 Peter 4:10).

Do you see that? We are to be *stewards* of God's grace. A steward is someone who manages the property or affairs of someone else. God wants us to serve his attributes to others—love, peace, kindness, and self-control, to name a few. If we who believe and love God don't pour out his love to others this season of the year, or at any time, who will? Even the way we choose to celebrate Christmas can be a gift of love that we bring to our world.

Are our choices of Christmas activities—and our attitudes—sending a positive message of hope, peace, joy and love, or are they sending a negative message of stress, chaos, and indifference? If those of us who love Jesus don't make a difference in how we celebrate the birth of our Savior, will things ever change? We may be the catalyst that frees others from the burden of perfection and expectations that keep them from fully reveling in the love and meaning of Christmas and enjoying their loved ones.

Today's Love Challenge: Start the circle. Draw close to God, listen to him, and talk to him. Ask him to pour his love into you and help you see opportunities to share his love and other attributes with others. When those opportunities come, reach out. Simple gestures of kindness speak volumes of love. I promise, love will be returned to you.

Further Reading: Luke 6:38, John 13:13-17, John 13:34, Romans 12:20-21, Romans 15:1-3, 2 Corinthians 9:6-10, Galatians 6:9, Hebrews 6:10, James 2:15-17

Day Four
Family

Many of us hope and fantasize about having a perfect family. We desire a warm, comfortable, loving interaction between members in the atmosphere of a peaceful home among people that we love. We want a place where we can relax, be ourselves, and enjoy each other and our life together.

Our family is where we seek our earliest and strongest desire for love, acceptance, and affection. It is also a place where we can receive out greatest wounds and disappointments. With the best of families there are hurts and differences that come with the territory. In reality, the perfect family doesn't, and never will, exist. There are always challenges, disappointments, hurts, and heartaches. These things are minimal in some families and consistent in others. Wherever your family is on that scale, you are not alone.

The unfortunate result of our culture's expectations of "family" during the holidays is often a painful dose of reality that exposes and reminds us of dysfunction, disharmony, or disconnection. If this is the case, the attempt of assembling your family for the holiday may be a daunting and disappointing task. On the other hand, this could be an exciting and rewarding time when families reconnect, differences are overlooked or accepted, and bonds are strengthened.

As we approach family gatherings that may have challenges, it is good to remember that the attitude and behavior of others is far beyond our control. We can only control our own attitudes, behavior, and choices. Many times our fantasies of perfection for our family can trip us up. What we hope for isn't always the reality of how things are or how they will turn out.

Accepting "what is" is much healthier than forcing or manipulating things into our vision and hopes. I don't mean in the sense of giving up hope for better relationships or being resigned to things never changing, but letting go of control or manipulation. We cause ourselves much grief and stress trying to get our loved ones to conform to our wishes, expectations, or to get along with each other. They are the captains of their ship—not us.

You may be surprised to know that Jesus had some family issues. We can take note of how he handled some interactions with them. In the early part of Jesus' ministry, his family tried to pull him away from the crowd while he was teaching because they thought he had lost his mind. It seemed they were embarrassed by him and didn't approve of the spectacle they thought he was making (see Mark 3:21-35). His brothers mocked him and didn't believe him (see John 7:1-5). I'm sure none of this was easy for Jesus, but he exercised boundaries and self-control in his interactions with his family. He didn't always cater to their demands or every wish, or let their attitudes influence him or his mission. Neither did he attempt to change their beliefs or their attitude toward him and what he was doing. No manipulation, no coercion, no pity parties, no demands. He simply loved them and accepted them where they were.

The lack of acceptance and validation from Jesus' family didn't stop him from living a productive and extraordinary life. He found the role of family fulfilled by like-minded believers and so can we (see Matthew 12:47-50). Jesus' family did eventually accept and believe his teachings and his divine appointment (see Acts 1:14).

In dealing with difficult family situations it's important to remember that we do have choices. The only control we have is what we do with those choices regarding our attitude, behavior, or actions. As we make those choices, it is always best to seek the Lord for what he desires of us in each situation.

Forgiveness is always God's requirement of us in any situation where someone has wounded or betrayed us. Reconciliation and restoration are not always possible, required, or even recommended, but love and forgiveness are not open for debate in God's eyes. Love and forgiveness may require any combination of humility, courage, acceptance, tolerance, boundaries, and hard choices.

In certain family situations we may need to say "No" in order to protect our priorities, our peace, our heart, or our well-being. Proverbs 4:23 (NIV) reminds us that, "Above all else guard your heart, for everything you do flows from it." That is so true because if our heart is struggling with pain, we are unable to be fully effective in anything that is before us or that God asks of us. A wounded or unforgiving heart consumes a great deal of our thoughts and energy and can cause us to make unwise decisions. Putting healthy boundaries in place with an attitude of love can help us protect our heart and our well-being. In preparation for doing so, it is very important for us to discern that our motive is pure and not out of spite or revenge. A pure motive can be making a choice not to put ourselves in the place of "victim," or it can be choosing not to take care of another person's responsibility. Maybe it's not saying "Yes" when we really mean "No", in order to protect our heart or our values.

God has called us to peace (see 1 Corinthians 7:15). In Romans 12:18 Paul says, "If it is possible (in some cases we may have to accept that it may not be), as much as depends on you, (what is in our control) live peaceably with all men" (parentheses mine). To live in peace doesn't mean we become doormats or relinquish our values, priorities, or self-worth. Living in peace means we love people, forgive them, and accept them with the same respect and love we give ourselves, relinquishing control and harsh judgment. A peaceful heart is found in those who can give value and love to others and to themselves equally and humbly.

Yes … it's up to us. Choices, changes, decisions. Seek God's wisdom to lead you. Rely on his grace to empower you to live out his desire for you and the interactions with your family.

Today's Love Challenge: Is there a family member who is a challenge or has wounded you? Is there tension or strife among members? Seek God's wisdom for what he wants from you concerning the situation. If you are blessed to have good, healthy relationships in your family, thank God for that amazing blessing.

Further reading: Psalm 133:1, Proverbs 22:24, Matthew 10:11-15, Romans 12:9-21, James 1:19-20, James 3:16-18, 1 Peter 3:8-12, 1 Peter 4:8-10, I John 2:10-11

Day Five
Forgiveness

Forgiveness is not the misguided act of condoning irresponsible, hurtful behavior. Nor is it a superficial turning of the other cheek that leaves us feeling victimized and martyred. Rather it is the finishing of old business that allows us to experience the present, free of contamination from the past.
~ Joan Z. Borysenko (azquotes.com)

How do you spell relief? That was a popular commercial slogan for a digestive aid a few years back. How do *I* spell relief? F-O-R-G-I-V-E-N-E-S-S.

How about you? Have you ever done or said something that caused harm or hurt someone and felt the exhilarating, liberating relief of their forgiveness? I have. Most of us have. It's a great feeling. It eases the agony of guilt and regret for the perpetrator and the weight of a grudge and bitterness for the forgiver. Both the act of forgiveness and receiving it are immensely freeing.

So why do we hold on to our hurts and disappointments from others? Why do we rehearse them until resentment builds and bitterness entraps us? We so easily become preoccupied with angry or vengeful thoughts that enslave our hearts and cause us to be ineffective as representatives of God's love. Our joy is suppressed as well. We want justice. We want revenge. And a little part of us wouldn't mind if they suffered a bit for the injustice or hurt they have inflicted on us.

Sometimes we're afraid that if we forgive it means we have to restore the relationship, or be reconnected with the person, and make ourselves vulnerable again. Restoring the relationship can be the outcome, if both parties involved choose it, but that is not a requirement of forgiveness. Forgiveness involves the choice to accept the consequences of another person's offense and leave the justice to God. Reconciliation and restoration aren't always possible since those outcomes require the willingness of both parties—and many times a great deal of change—not to mention that it may not always be safe or wise.

Forgiveness is a choice God requires us to make in order to remain in harmony with him and with others. As we forgive, we maintain a position to receive gifts of God's grace, (his divine influence) and his forgiveness. Hebrews 12:14-15 says this well: "Pursue peace with all people, and holiness, without which no one will see the Lord; looking carefully lest anyone fall short of the grace of God; lest any root of bitterness springing up cause trouble, and by this many become defiled."

We *fall short* of the grace God makes available to us by harboring unforgiveness and its by-product of bitterness. Holiness is the commitment of being fully devoted to God and what he requires of us. Forgiveness is one of those requirements. Bitterness will never become an issue if we can forgive. Clearly, bitterness causes great trouble, not only for the parties involved, but for many others that may be a part of our lives or that we interact with. It has a tendency to seep out into other situations and interactions. "The heart knows its own bitterness, and a stranger does not share its joy" (Proverbs 14:10).

Joy is consumed by bitterness. Set your heart and your mind free and employ the choice to forgive. The alternative has absolutely no benefit to anyone. Let's be conveyors of love and bring glory to God and peace to our lives.

Today's Love Challenge: Is there someone you need to forgive? Don't wait.

Further Reading: Matthew 5:43-44, Matthew 6:14-15, Matthew 18:21-35, Mark 11:25-26, 2 Corinthians 2:5-11

Day Six
Loving Self

A lot of us are pretty critical of ourselves. We're too short, too tall, to thin, too fat. We'd love a different nose or any kind of hair but our own. We've all done things we're not proud of or wish we could forget—or have a do-over. We botch up relationships, get ourselves in uncomfortable situations, and sometimes find ourselves alienated from others, wallowing in a sea of regret.

The Christmas season can magnify any remorse or condemnation we feel toward ourselves, especially if we find ourselves more alone than we'd like to be because of it. Whether condemnation is self-inflicted or hurled at us by another, it is painful and can be debilitating.

We've talked about forgiveness and the freedom that comes in releasing someone who has wounded us by giving up our need for revenge, but what about forgiving ourselves? Why do we torture ourselves with condemning thoughts that steal our gratitude and rupture our confidence? Why do we entertain negative thoughts of ourselves that zap our strength and minimize our effectiveness? Aren't those thoughts a form of revenge against ourselves? They certainly minimize joy and peace in our life. They cause us to lack the confidence and personal freedom necessary to truly reach out in love to others, mainly because we become too inwardly focused.

Jesus declared the second greatest commandment to be, "You shall love your neighbor as yourself" (Matthew 22:39). This commandment could have been given simply as, "Love your neighbor." However, every time it appears in the Bible, the love of self is a part of this admonition.

Can you see why?

If I don't believe I am valuable and worthy of love, I will, most likely, feel I have nothing to offer anyone else. My love well is dry, even for myself. How then can I give love? If I am confident of God's love for me, and that he values me, I am filled with his love and acceptance. This strengthens my confidence, and I have love that is eager to be shared. It is a natural occurrence that when we feel loved we want to give love, and when we give love we receive love from others. Self-condemnation stops this reciprocal process and represses our desire and ability to love freely and be loved. If we truly accept God's love and forgiveness, there is no place for condemnation. "There is therefore now no condemnation for those who are in Christ Jesus, who do not walk according to the flesh but according to the Spirit" (Romans 8:1).

As we confess our transgression and turn away from it, God forgives, and he holds no condemnation over us. Condemnation is sin's only *real* defeating power over us. It's not so much the sin that destroys our lives, it's the condemnation that comes with the consequence of sin. God tells us the power that condemnation once held is gone. Zero. None. He releases us from it. However, if we don't accept that release, the sin will continue to hold us in its grip. We are theoretically saying, "God, I know you are not holding this against me, but I feel it's necessary to continue to torture myself and avenge myself because of it, so I'm not going to accept the freedom you are offering." Ridiculous.

What God spoke to Israel through the prophet Isaiah is true for us because of the message of Christmas: Christ came to reconcile us and bring forgiveness.

"I have blotted out, like a thick cloud, your transgressions, and like a cloud your sins. Return to Me, for I have redeemed you" (Isaiah 44:22). To redeem means to sever, release, or preserve. We are released. We are free.

You are loved. Accept it. Celebrate it. Live like it. Love like it.

Today's Love Challenge: If there is any self- condemnation lurking in your thoughts, release them. Let them go. Accept God's forgiveness, love and freedom. Allow yourself to be set free.

Further Reading: Lamentations 3:20-24, Micah 7:18-20, John 3:16-21, John 15:15-17 Ephesians 1:3-6

Day Seven
Be Still

Be still and know that I am God.
~ Psalm 46:10

We have a hard time being still, don't we? Most of us feel compelled to be busy and on the move unless we're sleeping. Even in our sedentary moments, we're watching or reading or listening.

It's so hard to be still and take time to shut the world out for even a few moments, allowing ourselves to relax in a quiet and unhurried space of time. But it can be so refreshing. In the stillness God can speak to our hearts in enlightening ways.

It is the same for our interactions with people and loved ones. Those times when we break from our busyness and create time to give people our full attention are when we really get to know them. The spaces between our harried schedules are where intimacy happens and relationships deepen. We often go through our days and lives with no pauses and then wonder why our relationships may be falling apart.

Andy Stanley in his teaching study guide titled, "Take It to the Limit" says:

> "Margin is the space between your current performance and your limits. When you reach the

limit of your resources, strength, capacity, or self-control you have no margin. And without margin you have no room for error. The consequences of margin-less living are most apparent in our relationships. Love, intimacy, and friendship happen in the unstructured, unhurried world of margin. When we attempt to squeeze one more thing in, we inadvertently squeeze one more person out."

It is no different with our relationship with God. There must be time to be still, to pause, if we want to build intimacy.

God spoke through the prophet Isaiah and told us that a virgin would conceive a son who would be called 'Immanuel" which means: "God with us." He *is* with us. He is here for us. It's our part to move toward him to complete the relationship. I encourage you to do that by creating time to be still in order to focus on only him. Find a quiet place to be with him and give him priority. Schedule it into your day. Begin to create margins around your daily activities. Abandon the practice of scheduling things so tightly that there is no room for relationships to be nurtured and grow, or time for you to be still and refreshed.

God is with us, but too often we push him aside. We don't even recognize that he is there or that he is seeking our attention. In our hurry to move on to the next thing, and the next, and the next, we miss the refreshing, empowering, and loving nature of a relationship with him.

Take time, be still, and *know* that He is Immanuel … God with us.

"By this we know that we abide in Him, and He in us, because He has given us of His Spirit. And we have seen and testify that the Father has sent the son as Savior of the world. Whoever confesses that Jesus is the Son of God, God abides in him, and he in God. And we have known and believed the love God has for us. God is love, and he who abides in love abides in God, and God in him" (1 John 4:13-16).

Today's Love Challenge: Start practicing being still today. Just five minutes. I know Christmas is upon us, but it's five minutes that may make your day much easier! Find a quiet place, lock the bathroom door, take a walk, or jump in your car and park in a quiet place. Find your spot and just be still. Let this be a new beginning of a daily practice for the New Year.

Further reading: Psalm 62:5-8, Psalm 63:1-3, Psalm 91:1,

Closing Thoughts

Every aspect of life is about choice. How we choose to respond to God, to people, and to circumstances, will determine our peace, our contentment, and the level of our ability to navigate the hard places that life throws at us. Our choices have created our past and will determine our destiny. The Word of God instructs us to *choose* to seek him first and trust him. As we do this the cares and worries we have will be entrusted into his very capable hands. He will influence our weakness with the grace of his attributes, and our choices will be guided by his Spirit. May you celebrate your Christmas Day with joy, knowing he is with you, his Spirit is melded into yours, and his desire is for all things to work for your good as you trust him.

He is ... Immanuel.

Merry Christmas!

About the Author

Patricia lives in Western North Carolina. Her passion is to lead people to freedom and healing through God's truth. She has a special heart for preventing and freeing women from abusive and co-dependent relationships. She has served in Women's ministries, recovery groups, and has taught Bible studies for many years.